FEAR OF GOD

Fear of Food

A self-help programme for permanent recovery from eating disorders

GENEVIEVE BLAIS, M.S.W.

BLOOMSBURY

First published in 1995 by Bloomsbury Publishing plc, 2 Soho Square, London W1V 6HB

Copyright © by Genevieve Blais

The moral right of the author has been asserted

British Library Cataloguing in Publication Data

A CIP record for this book is available from the British Library

ISBN 0 7475 2024 0

10 9 8 7 6 5 4 3 2 1

Typeset by Hewer Text Composition Services, Edinburgh
Printed and bound in Great Britain by
Cox & Wyman Ltd, Reading, Berkshire

Other Health books available from Bloomsbury Publishing plc

Bloomsbury Encyclopedia of Family Health
Dr Robert Youngson
0 7475 2011 9

Bloomsbury Encyclopedia of Aromatherapy
Chrissie Wildwood
0 7475 2085 2

Cancer
What every patient needs to know
Dr Jeffrey Tobias
0 7475 1993 5

Candida
A practical handbook for sufferers
Angela Kilmartin
0 7475 2025 9

Running on Empty
Strategies for coping with ME
Kathryn Berne and Ann McIntyre
0 7475 2138 7

Funny Tummies
A practical guide to coping with digestive disorders
Dr Mile Whiteside
0 7475 2090 9

Holistic Women's Herbal
A complete guide to happiness, health and wellbeing at all ages
Kitty Campion
0 7475 2047 X

Medicines Third Edition
The comprehensive guide
Consultants: Dr Ian Morton and Dr Judith Hall
0 7475 2095 X

This book is dedicated to:

My family and friends who love me anyway, Walter for his continued support, and especially my Beloved Spiritual Teacher, Adi Da (the Da Avatar), whose wisdom has happily altered the course of my destiny.

ACKNOWLEDGEMENTS

I would like to thank the people who made this book possible: my agent Teresa Chris for her encouragement, good advice and belief in my work; my editor Rowena Gaunt for her vision and energy; and to all my clients who have shared so much with me.

I would also like to express my appreciation to my friends and family who have supported this work in their own special ways: my mother Genevieve Blair; my brother and sister-in-law David and Jody Blair; my sister and brother-in-law Loretta and Dick Wolf; my friends Ailsa Sargent, Brian Gelfer and Michael Wood. And finally, I would like to express my gratitude to my husband Walter Brew for always being there for me. He got me to the finish line.

CONTENTS

INTRODUCTION

Welcome to what may well be the singularly most effective book on recovery from compulsive eating available. There are no hyped-up strategies or gimmicks. The plain truth is that I have recovered from anorexia and compulsive eating and I'm going teach you how to do the same. I have turned my life into a success story and have helped others to do the same. I can teach you how to lose your obsession with food and balance your weight naturally by discovering the reasons that imprison you in this defeating cycle.

My experience comes from my work as a therapist in eating disorders for the past fourteen years. I obtained a Master of Social Work in 1981 so that I might help counsel others who suffer. In 1983, I was a part of a team that developed and ran the first eating disorders programme in Portland, Oregon, USA.

My success has come from twenty-three years of using my own body as a laboratory, from doing research and working with others. But mostly my success has come from being willing to release control and become ignorant about solutions. I am not thin nor am I fat. I am an ordinary person with an ordinary body. No one is going to be asking me to pose for fashion magazine covers. But I don't worry about food or my body. I am free of the obsession to be thinner and I am free from the fear of food and eating. And my weight is stable!

I began dieting when I was eleven years old. I took **amphetamines** (prescribed) on and off for eight years. Altogether, I have spent more than half my life losing or gaining weight and abusing my body in an effort to become slim. I used laxatives and vomiting as ways of purging extra calories. But mostly I dieted and binged, dieted and binged. As an adult, I have been every weight from seven and a half stone to fourteen and a half stone. I have been addicted

1

to sugar and been a compulsive overeater and exerciser. At one point, my determination and obsession to be thin resulted in an anorexic phase. Day after day, my attention was constantly on my body and what I was or wasn't going to eat. Dieting and low self-esteem consumed my days and nights. I thought of nothing but the day I would be thin. I never had a moment's peace and I never stopped feeling like an inadequate human being. I was a prisoner to my mind and body. It was bondage beyond belief. There were times when I wished I were dead. And times also when I knew I couldn't keep up the energy necessary to fight my fight any longer. When my weight finally peaked at fourteen and a half stone, I realised that none of my efforts would ever bring long-term success because my weight gains had very little to do with how I ate. I gave up dieting once and for all and began to lose weight. I have never dieted since, nor do I need to keep my weight in a normal range.

You too can live normally and naturally without compulsive eating or dieting and without gaining weight. If you follow carefully all the information and exercises in this book, there is no reason why you can't begin to change your life and your body. Believe me, I have covered every aspect that plays a part in keeping people stuck in the cycle of overeating and being overweight. Perhaps you don't even need to lose weight, perhaps you just need to learn to accept yourself as you are. By the time you have finished reading this book and doing all the exercises (mental, not physical) you should know exactly what it is that you need to do.

There are no simple answers to compulsive eating, just as there is no single strategy that can be applied for all to lose weight. Hundreds of books are written on dieting. Numerous psychological journals are filled with studies on obesity. No one has ever come up with a definitive cure for being overweight or curing compulsive eating. And that is because weight is as complex and diverse as the individual. In fact, disordered eating and weight have very little to do with food. They have a lot more to do with what people think of themselves, their perception of how they fit into the world and with loving and being loved.

Compulsive eating and weight difficulties are linked with a diversity of emotional and psychological states as well as genetic predisposition, learned behaviours about food and eating and the actual physical aspects of metabolism and the type of food eaten. Even self-knowledge is not the answer. You have been collecting everything you need to know for years, but knowing 'why' doesn't change anything either. You need to take that self-understanding and create an emotional/physical change. You need to integrate the mind and the body. This is a whole-body process. You need to learn how to work with your body as your friend and not as some problem that keeps hanging around. Essentially, all the information that you are going to need is already in your body and your mind. And what you don't know, I will either tell you or help you uncover.

This is a programme of recovery for all of those who have never been able to lose weight and keep it off permanently. For all those stuck in the cycle of compulsive overeating, for all those whose obsession with food and dieting takes up the greater part of each day. For all the overweight men and women who would just like to feel some peace and resolution with their own bodies. My experience is that you will never have to diet again to be the weight you want to be. You will not have to deprive yourself of food or torture yourself mentally. There is a much happier and freer way to live. There is the possibility of all this and more. Recovery from compulsive eating is possible!

Just remember that you are reading this book because you are ready to change your life. I'm not saying that it is going to be easy or that you can eat massive quantities of food and expect to be thin. You will have to devote time and energy and patience. But if I can do this, everyone can! If you are willing to put as much energy into this as you have given to dieting, then there is no way that you can fail. But it *will* take time.

This book is actually an extension of a course which I teach around the country in a seminar format. To get the most out of it, do not skip around. You need to follow it through systematically from beginning to end. It was written in this particular order for very good reasons. Each chapter is distinct and needs to be gone over thoroughly. The exercises throughout the book are extremely important. These are part of the 'how tos' that you have been looking for (although you should note that chapters 1, 2 and 14 have no Homework sections). Do take your time with them. You may even want to read the book all the way through first and then go back and slowly work your way through the exercises. But do them in sequence. And be sure and do the follow-up steps in chapter 13 to ensure your continued success. Compulsive people are notorious for being impatient. And that will be your biggest temptation. I know, because I am one of you! I also know that I can save you years of suffering and failure. I am going to teach you how to recover from compulsive eating so you never have to do this again. Isn't that worth paying attention to the details? Relax, breathe and enjoy!

Notes

- I have altered the names and some of the circumstances of my clients so as to maintain their anonymity. In some cases, I have made composites of a few different people or issues in order to do the same.
- Even though men do suffer from disordered eating as well as women and children can be girls as well as boys, I have refrained from using the politically correct referencing of 'she/he' to make the reading smoother.
- A word marked in **bold** in the text indicates that it is included in the Glossary.

1

chapter one

WHAT CONSTITUTES
AN EATING
DISORDER?

'Eating disorder' is a term that we are all becoming increasingly aware of. Most people these days either know of the term or of someone who has suffered or is suffering from an eating disorder. The Royal College of Psychiatrists estimates that at least one per cent of secondary-school girls suffer from full-blown anorexia, and another two to three per cent have partial syndromes. It is considered that at least two per cent of women between the ages of fifteen and forty-five suffer from full-scale bulimia, with another four to five per cent of this population having partial syndromes. The Eating Disorders Association reckons that the figures are much higher than these reported figures and that the numbers are nearer 150,000 to 200,000 sufferers of anorexia and bulimia in the UK at any given time. These figures do not include compulsive eaters or subclinical eating disordered persons. There are many more thousands of people who are compulsive eaters than the anorexics and bulimics put together, yet it is much harder to get statistics on this group. And often compulsive eating is not taken very seriously by the medical profession. Compulsive eaters are more apt to be considered greedy or lazy as opposed to someone who is suffering an actual disorder.

An eating disorder can be called by the name **anorexia**, **bulimia** or **compulsive overeating**. Even though the term used is 'eating disorders', they are not disorders of eating. In other words, the suffering and dilemma caused by an eating disorder is born out of a person's self-perception and not out of his or her desire or enjoyment of eating *per se*. It is not really about food initially, although, as the disorder progresses, it is the eating behaviour that seems to become prevalent. To the onlooker, this is certainly the case. But for the eating-disordered person, it is only the tip of the iceberg. In the USA, there is a new term for people with disturbed eating that doesn't fit in the clinical category of the first three; it is called 'subclinical eating disorder'.

The main prerequisites for saying someone has an eating disorder are as follows.

- There is a lack of acceptance of themselves that drives them to look for external ways of changing themselves so they can become acceptable.
- Instead of dealing with emotional or psychological issues, they distract themselves by putting all their energy into food, either eating or refraining from eating.
- They feel that their happiness is inevitably linked with their weight.
- They have an intense preoccupation with their weight and with the fear of gaining weight.
- This quest for thinness consumes the greater part of their waking moments.
- They generally feel out of control with their eating or remorseful and guilty when they eat.
- Weight loss or refraining from eating is viewed as an accomplishment. To them, it demonstrates that they have some type of control over themselves and their lives.

Essentially, if a person has developed an eating disorder, you can be sure that they are unhappy with themselves. Most link all of their difficulties to their weight. That is the beginning of their struggle; the rest of their actions develop from that pivotal point. Eating disorders cover a wide range of behaviours and dysfunction, but a great many of the issues and sensitivities are the same in each; they are simply dramatised in different ways. Let's take a look at each category of eating disorder and how they differ.

Anorexia

Sometimes referred to as **anorexia nervosa**. Literally, it means 'loss of appetite for nervous reasons'. However, this is not actually the case. Anorexics have not lost their appetite at all and often feel terribly hungry; but they do not allow themselves to fulfil their need for food. Their determination not to eat overrides their physical demands. It takes great will-power to deny themselves over a prolonged period of time (those of us who have ever tried even simple dieting know that this is not easy). In order to do this, they have to maintain very rigid methods (controls) on when and what they eat. They can develop some obsessively bizarre rituals in order to make themselves feel they have got it under control.

SOME COMMON SYMPTOMS

- Loss of twenty-five per cent or more of body weight.
- Cessation of menses (periods).
- Terror of becoming fat or gaining weight.
- Tendency to be a perfectionist.
- Downy hair growth on body.
- Poor circulation, sensitivity to temperature.
- Distorted body image.

STATISTICS

Generally, anorexia develops between the ages of fourteen and eighteen, though the age when children show the initial signs seems to be getting younger and younger. Some people develop it later in life. I developed anorexia in my late twenties. As many as ten to nineteen per cent of those with anorexia will die from either starvation or suicide.

A scenario of an anorexic may look like this: she is a young girl in a family of high achievers. She is anxious to please parents and others. She may appear, on the outside, to have her life under control and be confident about her abilities and what she intends to do. She sets very high standards for herself; is usually organized and tidy, and likes to have things go as planned. Often, as a younger child, she did not cause much disturbance, and was sometimes referred to as a 'good little girl'. On the outside, she can appear to be quite controlled, but on the inside often feels as if she is in the way, takes up too much space or is somehow inadequate. No matter how much weight she loses, it is not enough, and she probably still feels as if she is fat. I have never met an anorexic who was happy with the weight that she attained.

Bulimia

Bulimia is a condition characterised by eating large quantities of food and then **purging** either by vomiting or using laxatives or both. Often the bulimic has been able to keep this behaviour a secret for months or even years. Purging is the primary means of keeping weight under control. Because of this, bulimics often go unnoticed. Their weight doesn't tend to fluctuate in the way that an anorexic or compulsive overeater's does, though they can become quite bloated and swollen at times, given the amount of purging that they have become involved in. The purging is an important means of release for these people. Many become involved in purging as a way to cope with stress. First they eat, out of a compulsive need to feed, then they clean themselves out by either vomiting or taking laxatives. (And these people are not generally taking the recommended dosage – I have seen clients who have taken up to 200 laxatives a day.) The disturbance to the body can be tremendous. The act of purging completely destroys the body's water, salt and mineral balance. This is one of the reasons that they can become dehydrated or bloated and suffer serious digestion difficulties and organ failure.

SOME COMMON SYMPTOMS

- Eating massive quantities of foods (usually very high in calories) in one sitting and then ridding themselves of it by inducing vomiting or using laxatives.
- Obsessive, compulsive need to stuff a lot of food into themselves.
- Tendency to be chaotic or secretive in their behaviour.
- Fairly drastic mood swings.
- Chronic anxiety or depression.
- Chronic constipation or digestive difficulties.
- Dissolving of tooth enamel due to the acidity of bile from the stomach.

STATISTICS

Bulimia tends to develop in the late teens. Purging can cause a serious imbalance in the water, salts and mineral levels in the body. Bulimics can suffer heart attacks, swelling of the glands and/or a rupture in the oesophagus or stomach. They also experience the loss of enamel on the teeth due to the acidity of the bile from the stomach.

A picture of a bulimic might look like this: she is a university-age student, worried about her weight. She doesn't feel she has the control to diet in the long term, but wants to keep her weight down. She discovers that vomiting makes her feel cleaned out and thin and begins to use this method for controlling intake; but it gets out of control and her behaviour becomes more and more compulsive. There doesn't seem to be any way out. If she continues her out-of-control eating, she will get fat, so she must keep up the purging. She is caught in a trap with no way out.

Compulsive eating

Compulsive eating is often a term associated with greed or gluttony. Sometimes it is not taken seriously as an eating disorder. But anyone who has ever suffered will tell you that the mental turmoil and self-hate is as intense and destructive as any eating disorder. The difference between compulsive eating and anorexia is the lack of ability to deny eating over a long enough period to experience weight loss. The difference between compulsive eating and bulimia is the inability to bring themselves to purge. Otherwise many of the symptoms and characteristics are the same.

SOME COMMON SYMPTOMS

- Ardent preoccupation with weight and dieting.
- Inability to stop eating once started.
- Out-of-control eating not regulated by the body's natural signals of hunger, consumption of large quantities of food in one sitting or continuous eating.
- Perception of self as greedy and inadequate because of their failure to maintain their weight.
- Tendency to become overweight.

STATISTICS

Compulsive overeating can begin at any age. The act of dieting often promotes this type of behaviour because of continuous denial, and many health problems have been attributed to compulsive eaters because of the resulting weight gain. Research is now showing that overeating does not necessarily produce health problems, but in fact only exacerbates them once a condition is present.

There are no statistics showing the number of people suffering from compulsive eating, but one of the reasons why the Eating Disorders Association limits itself to anorexia and bulimia is because it knows that the response from compulsive overeaters would be too great to handle!

There is no definitive scenario for the compulsive eater. They come from a diversity of backgrounds, educational levels and socio-economic status. They come in every age and size. What we do know is that they suffer from a preoccupation with food and their weight, just like anorexics and bulimics.

Subclinical eating disorder

SED, or subclinical eating disorder, is a new term that has been coined in the United States. Given today's pressure on women to be thin, millions of women are preoccupied with their weight, though their behaviour may not be exaggerated enough to warrant being categorized as an eating disorder. These people (usually women) are now seen as having a subclinical eating disorder. They are usually women who are constantly dieting. They are preoccupied with perfecting the body. They may succumb to overeating, but not enough to produce large weight gains. They may use exercise to atone for their eating sins. But the one thing they surely have in common with all eating disorders is that they are not relaxed or happy about eating. Their relationship with food and their bodies has become a source of anxiety and not nourishment.

SOME COMMON SYMPTOMS

- Preoccupation with weight and body image.
- Unease about eating.
- Constant weight watching.
- Lack of bingeing or overeating to the same degree as a bulimic or compulsive overeater.

STATISTICS

In the United States, it is estimated that eighty to eighty-five per cent of women fall into this category. There are no statistics at this time about the percentage in Britain. Nor is there really a typical scenario for this type of person, but from the looks of the statistics, if you assume things to be fairly proportionate in Britain, then we are talking about a majority of the female population. Look around you. Do you know a woman who is happy about her body (as it is) or her weight?

The psychology of eating disorders

What causes a person to develop an eating disorder? The common characteristics and symptoms give us some clues to this. What we do know is that eating disorders are not really about food at all, but about a person being very unhappy with themselves and acting out ways of coping that produce additional distress. People undertake specific modes of behaviour because they see them as a solutions to their distress; they somehow think it will ease their pain or make things right. People generally do not pursue things because they are expecting them to make them unhappy. We are all trying to avoid pain and feel pleasure. The problem with disordered eating behaviour is that there is *no* pleasure to be derived from it.

It would be too easy to say, 'Oh, well, anorexia is caused by this or that.' People are individuals, and how they cope with life is unique to a certain degree. There is no single cause of eating disorders, just as there is no one course of treatment for all.

Disturbed eating behaviour is a form of coping. For the anorexic, it may be to feel that they have some control in their lives. I have heard other anorexics say that it is a means of getting some attention or nurturing. A lot of the bulimics that I have met are very highly functioning people. They are very busy people who feel they have a lot to juggle. On the outside, they seem to be able to handle a great deal. But on the inside, they feel at their wits' end and overwhelmed. The compulsive overeater is the one with the most social stigma attached. They begin from the point of view of being socially unacceptable and it goes from bad to worse.

When is it a problem and when is it a disorder?

The answer to that question is linked with the degree to which the eating disorder interferes with a person's life and how they live with it. It also has to do with the degree of exaggeration in behaviour. Someone who worries that they might have gained some weight over the holidays and then forgets about it come January is not a person with an eating disorder.

A good frame of reference is to note how much time each day is taken up with your preoccupation with food or weight. If you are spending the better part of your waking hours worrying about what you are eating/have eaten/are going to eat, if you are constantly berating yourself for your weight or what you have eaten, if you feel you are out of control with food, then you indeed have a real problem. Someone whose weight and preoccupation with food consume their days is someone who is distressed. If a person is bound by what they think of themselves and how they relate to food, then it is more than just a bit of a problem.

Where do you fit in?

Below is a questionnaire that can help you sort out just how much of a problem eating is for you. If you have answered 'yes' to four or more of these questions, then it would seem that you probably have an eating disorder.

1. Do you find yourself preoccupied with your weight on a daily basis?
2. Do you feel guilt or remorse after you eat?
3. Are you constantly trying to lose weight or alter your figure, either through dieting or exercise?
4. Do you hate your body?
5. Do you find yourself out of control with eating?
6. Are you fearful of certain foods?
7. Do you eat in secret?
8. Do you feel that your worth or success as a person is somehow attributable to your weight?
9. Does your weight or eating behaviour affect your social relationships?
10. Do you ever purge what you've eaten, either by using laxatives or by vomiting?
11. Do you ever eat until the point where you feel physically ill?
12. Do you find yourself hungry a lot of the time because you are withholding from eating?
13. Do you think you have a problem?

2 TREATMENT – WHERE TO START

I t is not easy to know exactly where to begin. The first thing you must establish is how much of a problem you have. This in itself can be elusive if you think you might have anorexia or bulimia, because one of the warning signs of either of these conditions is a denial that there *is* a problem!

The first thing to do is have a check-up with your doctor. Once you know what your basic health status is, then you can go to an expert in the field of eating disorders. But it is important to know if you have any type of physical complications that could present difficulties for you. It is also reassuring to know that you are basically healthy. A lot of people ask me how much damage they have done to their bodies by their compulsive eating, starving or purging; however, there is no way for me of knowing because I am not a trained medical practitioner. So go for a consultation first.

What has gone before

Eating disorders are not new, though they have certainly come to prominence much more in recent years. There have been numerous approaches to helping people with distressed eating, including behavioural programmes, psychotherapy, in-patient and out-patient programmes, nutritional counselling, the use of drugs to supplement therapy, family therapy, group therapy and self-help groups to name a few! To date, there doesn't seem to be any one **treatment milieu** that stands out as the most effective. One reason for this is that different types of treatment are beneficial for different conditions and difficulties. In recent years, doctors have been prescribing certain antidepressants to help people with bulimia and/or anorexia, though this would not be advisable for all people with symptoms of eating distress.

One method of treatment that is often used for anorexics is to put them in hospital for refeeding. In other words, they are required to eat a certain amount of calories per day to get their weight up quickly. This form of treatment is often not terribly successful, because many anorexics find the sudden weight gain too frightening and will lose the weight as soon as possible after leaving hospital.

I often find that the most common form of treatment for compulsive eaters is some type of controlled diet regime. I have never found this particularly useful in helping someone to overcome this disorder because it is often the fact that they have restricted themselves so much already that makes them go out of control. This solution only reinforces failure.

Different treatment approaches are often designed according to what is thought to be the primary presenting problem or factor. Therefore, the philosophy of a particular facility will define how they go about treatment. Family therapy is often used for young anorexics because they still live within the family unit, and it can provide a great deal of help for the family as well as the anorexic. Often a treatment programme will enlist a number of forms of treatment.

It is not easy to live with someone who is distressed about their eating because of their mood swings and insecurities. It is often advisable that people close to the sufferer (partners, spouses, parents, etc.) find a source of support for themselves as well. There are some self-help groups that include carers as well as sufferers in their meetings, which enables everyone concerned to gain some understanding and support. For information about self-help groups around the country, you can ring the Eating Disorders Association, listed in the Helpful People section at the end of the book.

Types of help available – complementary and conventional

There is help available for all eating disorders, though not as many formal programmes for compulsive overeaters and subclinical eating-disordered people. Throughout Britain, there are NHS programmes as well as private hospital programmes and individual therapists for the treatment of anorexia and bulimia. Some NHS programmes also work with compulsive eaters, but you are more likely to find counselling centres or individual therapists that are more suitable for people with this difficulty. The treatment will vary according to the philosophy of the therapist, which is why it is very important that the type of treatment you undertake should depend on what you (or your eating-distressed person) feels the most comfortable with and what fits your circumstance the best. Some people feel very uncomfortable in group situations, so it is unlikely that that type of setting would be very helpful.

Some people find alternative therapies useful in aiding their recovery. These include acupuncture, aromatherapy, assertiveness classes, homeopathy and massage. You can locate these therapies in the Yellow Pages. Health-food stores often have information about local alternative practitioners as well. It is unlikely that alternative therapy alone would be enough to help overcome compulsive eating, though it can be a pleasant way to augment your primary form of treatment. For instance, learning to relax with yourself and your body can be very important in promoting recovery, so anything that you can do to help you advance in this way would be beneficial. Compulsive eaters are notorious for not spending time and energy on themselves, so a nice, weekly massage could be of great benefit. Not only would it help you to relax, but it also helps you to reassociate with your body and feel good about it.

Again, look in the Resources section (page 193) to find suggestions for treatments and referrals.

Can I ever be different?

Absolutely! You are completely retrainable. Your recovery depends on:

- recognising that you have a problem;
- being willing to devote time and energy to your own recovery;
- getting some support and help for yourself.

There is no reason why you shouldn't be able to recover if you want it enough, though the process may be uncomfortable at times. But then, isn't suffering compulsive eating uncomfortable? And from experience, both personal and professional, I can tell you that people who get themselves some support have a better chance of recovery than those who don't. The sooner you can get some help the better.

Approaching your GP

Doctors vary a great deal in their knowledge and sympathy for compulsive eaters (and other eating-disordered people, for that matter). I shudder to tell you how many stories I have heard from clients who, when they went to their doctor, received the response, 'Well, just pull your socks up and get on with it!' However, even if your doctor does not know much about the problem him- or herself, he or she may well be able to refer you to someone who specialises in this area. It is also very helpful, as I said earlier, to get the benefit of a physical check-up before proceeding with anything.

Go to your doctor expecting that he or she will be able to offer you some type of help, even if it is just to tell you about a programme or therapist. Your doctor could be quite valuable for certain programmes that require medical recommendation.

Beginning a programme of recovery

Really take your time to find out what type of treatment is available for you, what it will cost you (if anything) and what philosophy is behind it. This will save you frustration and valuable time. There are always some dubious professionals around who may promise a quick cure, hype results or try to disguise the likely cost of treatment, so be discriminating. There is a good deal of variance in both the treatments and the ways they are offered.

I would suggest you find a therapist who specialises in eating disorders and/or a self-help group. It could definitely be to your advantage to utilise both avenues at the same time. This way, you get the benefit of some individual attention to work privately on issues that are personal and you also meet other people who are in the process of recovery. One factor that is important in recovery is knowing that you are not alone and people *do* progress and recover!

3

WEIGHT OBSESSIONS

How do you measure success?

Before we begin the self-help information, let me ask you something. What do you expect from this book? Are you expecting that, after reading this, you will magically be able to stop eating compulsively? Are you hoping that somehow weight will just drop off overnight? Are you looking for a miracle cure? If you are, then you might as well put this book down now because you will be disappointed.

This course is not about magic, but about long-term success. It is about coping with life as it is. It is for people who seriously want to change their lives and their weight. The two must go together – our bodies do not operate in a vacuum. You can alter your eating behaviour in a variety of ways, but if you never address the reasons that it got out of balance to begin with, you are doomed to fall back into the trap. You need to look at your whole life, not just your eating or your body. Instead of asking yourself, 'How do I stop being out of control with food?', ask yourself, 'What is it that I want from food?'

We also need to look at what you consider success. Is success just about losing a few pounds? Does it have to do with having some peace of mind about your body and food? Would success for you be losing obsessional cravings and overeating patterns? If you could feel happy with your body and enjoy the food that you eat, would you really mind exactly what size you were? What does success look like for you? If you don't know where you are going, how will you know when you get there?

We set ourselves standards in every area of our lives. We decide that, if we meet those standards, then we are successful. We associate things, people and certain behaviour with those standards, then make sweeping generalisations about them. And we use these generalisations to compare ourselves to others. We attach value and morals and judge everything as if it could all be measured. We act as though we have to compete in life to get the ultimate reward. Which is what? Being thin? Is that it? What happens after you get thin? Do you really think you will be able to accept yourself thin if you didn't like yourself fat?

What exactly is the problem?

Very early on in life, I began measuring my worth in relationship to my body. I didn't get teased a lot about my weight until I was ten or so. I don't think I even thought about it much. But I was still beginning to take on the belief that weight was connected with being valued and accepted. I thought that my problem with being a successful person had to do solely with what my body looked like and what size it was. I thought my weight was my biggest problem in life. But that was just a symptom of my unhappiness. I was unhappy first. Then I got unhappy about my weight. But I still thought my weight was my primary problem. And because I started to focus on my weight being a problem, I also started to focus on my eating as a problem. I began to deprive myself of food in order to fix my body problem.

What I do know for certain is that neither your weight nor your eating behaviour is your primary problem. Your primary problem is that you are unhappy with yourself. This is not to say that you have some deep-rooted psychological difficulty and that you need to go through years of psychoanalysis before anything will change. Nor are you seriously disturbed or need to be put away! You are simply unhappy, and it is showing up on your body as weight (or mental agonising over your weight) or out-of-control eating. The natural process of the body to receive and release has become unbalanced. One of your biggest problems has been that you have been brainwashed into thinking that dieting is the answer to your unhappiness and your weight. Powerful social conditioning leads us to expect that the only way to lose weight is by dieting and that this is the only solution; if we weren't so greedy, we would just get on with it. However, nothing could be further from the truth. If you begin to realise that weight and eating are as complex and individual as you are, then you will understand that no amount of dieting can give you the results that you want. Besides, dieting doesn't even work for keeping weight off. Let's look at the reasons for this.

The diet trap

If you are like most of us, you have undertaken numerous diet schemes in order to lose weight. The common factor that links us together is that, for the great majority of us, dieting failed to produce any long-term results. If diets worked, we would have all gone on only one in our lifetime, and that would have been the end of it! Dieting actually helps to create compulsive eating. Most compulsive eaters are also seasoned dieters.

The grim facts are that ninety-five per cent of dieters regain their lost weight. Yet sixty-six per cent of British women diet sporadically, and fifteen per cent are on permanent diets. To add insult to injury, the 1983 Royal College of Physicians' Report on Obesity stated that British men and women are getting fatter, despite the fact that they have been eating a steadily decreasing number of calories since 1960. This is also the case in the United States. People have more wealth, more convenience foods and more diets to choose from, but the average person is getting larger in size.

I often hear failed dieters rebuke themselves for not having sufficient will-power to stick to a diet. Yet I have never met a group of people who are more determined to do the same thing over and over again, even though they don't get the results they want. If that isn't will-power, I don't know what is! (Unless it's just pure masochism!) If you were given a task at work that you knew you couldn't accomplish and you were given it week after week, at some point you would either go crazy or have to stop! No one can put up with that type of constant failure over and over again. So why are you so willing to keep going for the next diet?

Why diets fail

There are some very specific reasons why diets cannot give you permanent weight loss. The first and foremost of these is that dieting lowers yours metabolism. When you don't give your body enough nutrients for it to survive, it has to take matters into its own hands. Since the body doesn't know what you're going to give it or when, and if you are consistently giving it too little (as with dieting), it must maximize its usage of what you *do* give it. So the body begins to process food more slowly. It takes its time so it can maintain continuous energy for you. In some ways, you could say that your body becomes more efficient when you diet. It uses less and less to keep you functioning. And the more you diet, the more you disrupt your metabolism. 'Dieting reduces the metabolic rate by an astounding fifteen to thirty per cent and reduces the number of calories expended during activity . . . This compensation is found in both normal-weight and overweight dieters' (Garner and Garfinkel, 1985).

Everything slows down when you diet, not just your metabolism. It is very common in anorexics (whose bodies are in a perpetual state of starvation) that all their vital organ functions slow down. This is so the body can maintain life. It is also extremely common for anorexics, when they begin to put weight back on, to put on more than might be expected. This is because it takes time for the body to adjust itself to its natural 'set point'.

Everyone's body has a weight where it naturally wants to stabilise. This is called the **set point**. With dieting, we are constantly trying to alter this set point. This confuses the body a great deal, and it tries to fight against it. You can gradually alter your set point through exercise (which we will talk about later), but most people try to do it radically and quickly with dieting. You are only looking for trouble if you try it this way. It sets up a conflict between you and your body. When you start overriding your body's natural cues, you make it even more difficult for your weight to stay balanced.

> *I know that if I hadn't started trying to lower my natural set point, I wouldn't have had so much trouble with gaining and losing weight over the years. I am basically the same weight now as when I was a teenager. I tortured myself for years with undereating and overeating and took amazing detours with my weight. And at the end of the day, I let my body go to the weight it wanted to go naturally. Guess where it went? It went straight back to my early adult weight. Without, I should add, my trying to manipulate it. You see, I could have saved myself years of torment and hundreds of pounds (in both sterling and body size) by working with my body where it was to begin with!*

Dieting in itself doesn't seem like a problem, it seems like a solution. The problem really begins when you decide that you've had enough starvation (dieting) and want to eat normally again. The body hasn't had any time to readjust itself to your new plan. It has only just adjusted itself to being starved. Besides, it doesn't have any reason to believe that you are now going to be consistent with it and feed it properly. To protect itself, when it first sees food coming in, it will hoard it, set it aside, just in case you are not going to give it anything else. Because we have lowered our metabolism, anything that we eat will be processed more slowly. This will lead to weight gain, which is exactly what we were trying to avoid in the first place! Erratic eating behaviour really upsets the body. Then, of course, we get angry with our own bodies because of the weight fluctuations when all they were trying to do was keep us alive.

Logically, it makes sense that dieting lowers the metabolism. Science is finally beginning to admit this. Personally, I think you have 'road tested' enough diets to know that they don't work. It isn't necessary for you to continue to put yourself through such an ordeal. It only works against you. Instead you must learn to work *with* your body.

LOSE WEIGHT – STOP DIETING!

One of the hardest things is convincing people that they really won't go completely out of control if they quit dieting. There is no way for me to convince you of this with rational argument. *I* know it is true because I have pushed through this fear. I didn't quit dieting because I found out that it lowered my metabolism. I didn't have this information at the time. I didn't quit dieting because I thought it wasn't a good idea any more. I quit dieting because I was desperate. I had nothing else to lose. My best dieting efforts had just resulted in a weight of fourteen and a half stone. I was miserable, and dieting had put me there. So I didn't care anymore. I was willing to risk going out of control if I quit dieting. But exactly the opposite occurred. Since I didn't care about dieting anymore, I wasn't anxious about my weight or food. I became more relaxed. And as I became more relaxed, I changed how and what I ate. I had no more reason to overeat because I knew I could eat whatever I liked whenever I wanted. I have seen others do it and I have seen the difference that it has made. But you must experiment for yourself, because this fear of losing control is one of the major emotions that will block your recovery.

About a year after a client named Maria took my seminar, she rang me up and said, 'Guess what I've done this summer?' I said, 'I don't know, what have you done?' and she said, 'I lost two stone!' I was afraid to ask her how she had done it, but I enquired anyway, and she said, 'Well, I didn't do it by dieting! When you used to tell me that I could lose weight without dieting, I didn't believe you, and it has taken me a long time to realise that what you said was true. I was afraid that if I quit dieting, I would go completely out of control with food. But I didn't, and now I do believe you, because I quit dieting and lost this weight'.

DEPRIVATION MENTALITY

Another reason that dieting doesn't work and sets us up to eat compulsively is because it makes us feel deprived. It conditions us to feel we have to suppress what we desire. We think of ourselves as separate from the rest of the human race. We don't believe that we can eat the same kinds of food as others. We feel we have to go without. This type of thinking only produces anxiety and pressure. I call it **deprivation mentality**. It is this very state of mind that propels people to go to extremes in their eating behaviour. Essentially, we become like pressure cookers. Fairburn and Wilson, in their book *Binge Eating, Nature, Assessment and Treatment*, recognise that dieting, or severe limitation of food, is exactly part of what predisposes a person to binge. If you feel that you can't have what you really want and you have to restrain yourself, you are accumulating significant tension. At some point, you are not going to be able to sustain all the energy and feelings that have backed up. You are going to have to release them. Either we feel we can't stand the rigid control any longer and/or we want to be like everyone else. You are going to want to get your own back. Unfortunately, the central way that we tend to rebel is by eating compulsively! Don't tell me that compulsive eating is not self-destructive. It is. We finish by hurting ourselves instead of looking after ourselves. At the end of the day, we punish ourselves with the one thing that we imagined would bring us pleasure.

This deprivation mentality encourages compulsive reasoning. I'm sure that on occasion, you've told yourself, 'Well, since I can never ever eat chocolate again, then I must eat every bit in sight' or 'I must eat everything that I like today, because tomorrow I will be changing the rest of my life, I'm going on a diet and I can never eat the things I want again!' How many times have we fallen into that frame of mind and how many times have we been disappointed with ourselves for not being able to keep the vows we made to ourselves? There is no reason why anyone should feel bad about themselves for not being able to keep such unrealistic and unreasonable goals.

There is no reason why you can't have the same foods as others. No one can live under the constant punitive restrictions we impose upon ourselves. When I say that there is no reason why you shouldn't be able to eat whatever you like, people generally get scared. They translate 'You can eat whatever foods you like' into 'I can constantly overeat'. No wonder they don't believe me! That isn't what I said! You can eat whatever you want and not have to diet to maintain normal weight only if you eat when you are actually hungry. You can't overeat day after day and expect to be thin! But if you allow yourself to eat what you really want and feel that it is readily available, you will lose the obsession to eat compulsively. Eating what you want works! In fact, it is the very first thing you must tackle or you won't be able to move on to the next steps of freedom from compulsive difficulties. If you don't break out of this oppressive philosophy, you will feel that you are constantly on some kind of diet. Don't you want to be free from food obsessions, free from worrying about your weight, free from feeling bad about yourself? You must stop feeling that you cannot have what everyone else has. You must start eating like ordinary people.

THE CYCLE OF FAILURE

There are two other reasons that dieting does not work. One very important reason is because it fosters a cycle of failure. We have already established that you cannot possibly keep weight off after dieting. You put the weight back on, so you think that you've failed. You didn't fail, the diet failed. But your mind grabs hold of the negative results and plays them back to you over and over again. This just reinforces a negative self-image. This doesn't help you, this makes you feel worse about yourself, and the last thing you need is to feel worse about yourself. You are much too quick to blame yourself.

Dieting also promises quick fixes to problems that have little or nothing to do with your body, so again you will fail. Dieting addresses the body only on a certain physical level. But human beings are much more complex than that. Everything that we are is interwoven between the body, mind and spirit. You can't separate the body from the mind, so if you apply a solution only to the physical aspects of the body, you have compartmentalised the results. The body will not maintain anything if the rest of you isn't in harmony with what is going on. Most of us who struggle with our weight dismiss the body as something different from ourselves. If this is your attitude, you can't possibly expect to achieve a lasting change. I will address such aspects of hidden emotional conflicts that keep you stuck in a later chapter.

The facts about being overweight

I would like to give you some background information to help you understand obesity and the body in general. Clinically, a person is considered obese if they are thirty per cent or more above their ideal body weight. As I have stated before, establishing your ideal body weight is a very individual matter. But I'm sure you know if you are just a bit overweight or if you would be considered obese. Basically, there are two types of obesity: hyperplastic and hypertrophic.

HYPERPLASTIC OBESITY

Hyperplastic obesity is a term used to describe the weight problem of someone who became overweight during their child-hood. When children are growing up, their bodies continue to produce cells until they reach their physical maturation level. For girls, this is usually about age fourteen and for boys it is usually about age eighteen. This means that they continue to grow in height and weight and to develop sexually until the body says they have become adults. At this point, their growth slows down dramatically and almost stops. If you overfeed children while they are still in this growing stage, their bodies will produce more and more fat cells. By the time their bodies stop growing, they may be running around with seventy million more fat cells in their bodies than their normal-weight friends. This is clearly a set-up for future difficulty in trying to keep their weight at a normal level, because the body wants to feed all those extra fat cells.

It does seem more difficult for people who became overweight as children to lose weight and keep it off. However, do not let this put you off. I was one of those fat kids, and it is completely possible. It just takes a little more retraining of the body.

HYPERTROPHIC OBESITY

Hypertrophic obesity is a term used to describe the condition of someone who has become overweight as an adult. What this means is that the body does not produce *more* fat cells, it simply takes the ones you already have and expands them. Essentially, that is what happens when you gain weight. The existing fat cells in your body fill up. Weight is not something that comes and goes. It is the expanding or shrinking of the fat cells.

To help you get in touch with just how you see yourself in relation to your body, here is a questionnaire for you. Choose the answer that most fits how you feel about yourself.

1. I . . . my body.
   a love
   b feel all right about
   c ignore
   d hate

2. My weight is . . . to me.
   a extremely important
   b very important
   c quite important
   d not really important

3. My body is . . .
   a wonderful.
   b acceptable.
   c a nuisance.
   d disgusting.

4. If I could change my body I would alter . . .

5. My body is . . .
   a my friend.
   b my enemy.
   c a problem that I can't seem to work out.

6. My eating is . . .
   a no problem.
   b sometimes difficult.
   c out of control.

7. I want to please . . . with my weight.
   a others
   b myself

8. I expect to . . . with my weight.
   a be successful
   b fail again

Would it surprise you to know that, when I give this questionnaire to my clients, most of them answer that they either ignore or hate their bodies? They also generally indicate that they see their bodies as some type of problem that they just can't seem to control. The answers invariably lean towards negative self-imaging. Most people with eating disorders or weight difficulties feel quite dissociated from their bodies and view them in negative terms. How did you answer?

HOMEWORK

A note about the homework sections. These are very important. Whether you feel you have thought about the answers before or not, it is important that you take the time to write down your thoughts. It is worth spending time clarifying in your own mind what it is you do and believe. The homework is intended to help you collect useful data so that you can proceed to alter those things that keep you stuck. Before you can fix anything, you need to know what's wrong! Some of your answers may surprise you.

PRACTICAL STEPS

- Do a food inventory of your house. What kinds of food do you keep in your house? Do you like the food you have or do you just keep food you feel is good 'diet food'?

- What kind of food do you like? You need to start eating food that you like, not food that you think you should eat or food that you think will help you

lose weight. You need to break into your deprivation mentality.

- Begin to practise guilt-free eating. Eat only when you are actually physically hungry. When you are hungry, allow yourself to eat whatever takes your fancy. You have felt deprived for long enough — there is no reason why you can't enjoy the same foods as other people. If you feel you want to eat nothing but chips or ice-cream or biscuits for a fortnight, do it! Remember, eating what you like is not the same thing as eating until you feel ill! But do not deprive yourself. For now, you need to eat what you want, enjoy it and not feel guilty! This is the very first step in breaking out of the deprivation mentality.

WRITTEN EXERCISES

1 Write down all the different diets you have ever gone on. What happened after you went off them? Is there any

31

part of you that believes that dieting will still work for you? How many more times do you need to fail at dieting to decide that it is not really a solution?

2 Write down all the different weights you have been. Did any of them seem as if they were easy to maintain without effort? What weight does your body naturally tend to drift back to? Do you have an idea of what your body's natural set point might be?

3 Do you think that you are a compulsive eater or do you think you've just had some hard luck with your weight?

4 In what ways does your eating interfere with your life and your happiness?

4

THE MODERN
DOUBLE BIND

> *'From the beginning of time, the human race has had a deep and powerful relationship with food – if you eat you live, if you don't you die. Eating food has always been about survival, but also about caring for and nurturing the ones we love. However, with the added stresses of modern life, it has now become an expression of how we feel about ourselves and how we want others to feel about us.'*

[From a speech given by HRH The Princess of Wales to the International Conference *Eating Disorders '93*, 27 April 1993.]

In this day and age, a lot of importance is given to first impressions and what people look like. People are attracted to and judged immediately by appearance. We live in a society preoccupied with looking good and feeling good, exploiting experiences and sensations. We are trying to turn the body into something sexy that will provide fulfilment and happiness. Adverts and social pressure convince us that being slender will bring lasting happiness and a panorama of experiences and advancement. And, in some ways, it is absolutely true that the size of your body will bring different possibilities your way. There are many vocations that are only available to certain sizes. For some of these careers, it is obvious that an overweight person might not be the best suited for the job. But for others, it may be plainly subjective discrimination that has nothing to do with practicalities. Sometimes you will never know if your weight has been a limit for you. Discrimination and ignorance about being overweight are rampant. And what is worse is that we take on board such attitudes and turn against ourselves!

Cosmopolitan magazine surveyed over 7,000 of its readers to find out their feelings and attitudes about food and body image. The results were printed in an article entitled 'Your Love-Hate Relationship with Food'. Though some of the questions had to do with food and eating, part of the questionnaire concerned itself with social and personal opinions of acceptance. Nearly half the respondents felt they were 'inadequate' in comparison to the way women are presented by the media. But those same women (and more – sixty-eight per cent of the total) had no sympathy for those overweight people who did not fit into this social ideal. In fact, they felt that overweight people were 'weak willed'. Ninety-seven per cent said that noticing other women's figures had a lot to do with being dissatisfied with their own body. And ninety-one per cent said that they envied other women's looks. The survey also reported that the more women dieted, the more unhappy they became and the more contempt they had for themselves.

Learn to love your body

We treat our bodies like problems, as if they were an enemy following us around. We act as if we are not part of our bodies and often live from the neck up. We imagine that everything can be accomplished through the mind. We avoid looking at our bodies or feeling them to be a part of us in any positive way. How many times have you passed a mirror and decided that you could only look at the upper portion of your body? Does looking in the mirror bring up self-criticism? Perhaps you don't even have any full-length mirrors in your house. I know many overweight and eating-disordered people who only consult a mirror to put on their make-up or style their hair. They think that if they ignore their body, somehow they don't have to worry about it. They think that ignoring it will lessen their emotional turmoil. In this way, we are constantly fighting against ourselves. How can you expect your body to co-operate if you hate it? Who or what are you actually hating? You really need to stop and think about that one. Our problem is not our weight or our eating habits; our problem is that we despise ourselves, seemingly because of our weight. But our *real* problem is with low self-esteem and dissociation. We let the faceless masses of advertising determine our worth.

We need to learn to have compassion with ourselves and love our bodies as part of who we are. This does not mean that you have to like the fact that you are overweight or like how your body looks. But you do need to accept your body as a part of yourself and see that it is trying to tell you something by being overweight. Your body is very unhappy, and you need to pay attention to it. We tend to be much nicer to our friends than we are to ourselves. If you treated your friends in the same way as you treat yourself, you probably wouldn't have very many friends! Your weight is not your problem or your worth. You are distracting yourself with this notion.

Begin to get familiar with your body. You need to do things that make you feel good, good in *your* body. Start building up positive associations with your body. You can do this in any number of different ways. Have a massage, go swimming, have **aromatherapy**, paint your toenails, get a new hairstyle, whatever appeals to you. You have built up many negative associations with how your body feels and you don't think of your body in positive terms; this has to change. Put the book down and make a list of things that you like to do physically and that make you feel good. Don't be surprised if this is not very easy to accomplish. It may take you a while to develop a list. Perhaps you need to explore and experiment with many possibilities. But once you have this list, you can refer to it whenever you are bored or feeling bad about yourself or wanting to eat for no apparent reason. If you have the list handy, you won't even have to think about what you can do to turn your circumstance around. This is particularly helpful if you're in a confused or anxious state. Simply follow what you have written down and then see how you feel.

Responsible eating

I often hear overweight people say that they don't eat as much as other people (apart from when they go on a binge). I know that this is true because I fit into the same category. We have made our bodies less efficient by dieting so much. I have had to retrain my body how to utilise food. And I still can't eat mountains of food whenever I want. Nor do I want to. I don't go hungry, nor do I eat foods that don't appeal to me. I eat tasty food! So what if I can't eat continuously all day long? What is so appealing about eating massive quantities of food? Why do people feel envious of others who can eat limitless amounts? Is it fun to eat until one feels unwell? Again, holding back from having what you really want makes overeating look like fun.

THINK ABOUT WHAT YOU EAT

Most overeating is done unconsciously. We don't pay attention to what we are doing because it's just too painful. We are people who already have low self-esteem and extremely high expectations. We are constantly watching ourselves in a very critical way. Watching ourselves eat compulsively only adds to the disgust that we feel. But we need to wake up to what we are doing. We cannot continue to go through life asleep. We must make eating a choice and not a coincidence.

Take some time to think about what your eating has been like in the past week. Did you feel you should have started a diet because it's what you have always done? Do you believe that it's possible to eat what you want and not gain weight? You see, if you are relaxed about food and really allow yourself to eat whatever you want, you won't feel you are always depriving yourself. Therefore, you will release the need to binge, sneak eat or overeat. Compulsive eating, which is really unconscious eating, stems from anxiety, not from feeling balanced or rested. Making smart choices about eating is not the same as suppressing desires.

What have you observed about yourself recently in relation to your eating? We need to become rigorously honest about what we do and what we eat. It is hard to take a look at what we actually do with food, because it makes us feel bad about ourselves all over again. But it is very important that we are honest with ourselves so we can get a clear picture of our situation. And we desperately need to develop compassion for ourselves. We have to get out of the way of thinking that we are either good or bad depending on what the scales say or what our behaviour with food has been. People who eat compulsively treat themselves as if they have committed some grievous crime. They act as if they should repent in some way for the rest of their lives. Eating or overeating is *not* a crime! And as Shelley Bovey aptly named her book, *Being Fat Is Not a Sin*. What you eat or how much you eat has no bearing on your goodness as a person. You are not wicked or stupid because of what you put into your mouth. Compulsive eating is simply a behaviour that is maladaptive to our needs and it doesn't do us any good.

Gaining weight is easy

Putting on extra weight can be so easy and so subtle that people may not even notice they've done it until it's too late. Gaining weight after coming off a diet is inevitable. And this weight gain does not mean that you were overeating or eating more than 'ordinary amounts' to produce the extra poundage. Remember the body rebels against dieting. The more you diet, the more your body will fight against weight loss. The body is naturally smart. It doesn't like dieting! Physical activity can also play a role in suble weight gain. There have been studies following simple daily activities in relation to weight gain. For instance, in one study, women who were typists working on manual typewriters and who were upgraded to using electric typewriters gained about twelve pounds in a year. And that was just from reducing their activity while typing. It seems like such a small amount. But everything adds up!

It takes 3,500 calories to make one pound. So it follows, then, that if you increase your daily intake by only a hundred calories per day, in thirty-five days, you would gain one pound. Think how easy this is to do! One hundred calories is not very much at all. You could achieve this increase just by adding an extra tablespoon of fat or salad cream per day.

UNCONSCIOUS EATING

Is your eating unconscious? Are you eating hidden calories that put weight on easily? Are you adding that extra hundred calories per day without noticing it? Do you have a drink or two a day? Or maybe five or six at the weekends? Alcohol is the highest calorie per gram substance that we can put in our bodies. It is a way of taking on a lot of extra calories without filling up the stomach. Eating high-calorie foods that go down fast can also sabotage you. They go down so quickly that the stomach doesn't have much time to tell the head that it's full. Think about it. What foods are consumed the fastest? Vegetables and grains? Or ice-cream, sweets and creamy things? It is very easy to eat a lot of high-calorie items in a short period of time. It takes a lot longer to eat whole foods that take time to chew. What fills you up more? What is more satisfying to the body? What types of food do you tend to eat compulsively? Do you feel deprived if you haven't had peas or carrots for a few days? Then why do you feel deprived if you haven't had ice-cream for a week?

WHAT FOOD DOES YOUR BODY WANT?

We must get into the habit of observing what type of food choices make us unhappy. Not because some diet scheme has said that certain foods are forbidden or bad and if we eat them we should feel guilty. There are no 'good' or 'bad' foods. I cannot say this enough times. It must become like a **mantra** in your head. You are not a virtuous or sinful person for what you eat or don't eat. Food is just food! The only thing it can do is take away hunger and nourish the body. It is not your mum or love or anything magical. It is just food. Food cannot control you. It cannot chain you to a chair and force itself down your throat! You must choose to eat it or not eat it. It is the same with how much you eat. You must take back your control. You are in charge of what you put in your mouth.

Your body will respond to whatever you put into your mouth. It will react in one of four ways.

- It might feel satisfied that you fed it something that it needed.
- It might feel ill because it has been stuffed too full or ingested something that it considers toxic.
- It might keep looking for more of the same because the food has an addictive quality to it.
- It will be disorientated because your selection is inadequate.

When the body receives what it considers nourishment, it will let you know by being happy. It will say 'ahh, thanks, that hit the spot'. I'm sure you have all experienced this sensation. You know you've put exactly the right food in. When the body doesn't like what you've put in, it will become disagreeable. You might get flatulence or acid stomach or heartburn. And I'm sure that you have felt how the body responds when it is stuffed full of too much or the wrong kind of food. It feels ill. The body also gets dazed when addictive-type foods are absorbed. It produces neurotic impulses that it must have more – more of the addictive food. Have you ever noticed that sometimes those 'forbidden foods' leave you feeling frustrated or empty right after eating them? That's because the body doesn't get any real nutrition. It is still looking for the real food to come down. Often people continue to eat compulsively because of this feeling of not being nutritionally satisfied. The body is in a state of longing, so we go on looking for things to appease it; only it never gets satisfied if we're putting empty calories into it. Junk foods do not feed the body, and your body knows the difference.

'PICKING'

Another familiar way of eating compulsively is by picking your way through the day. Picking (or grazing, as some call it) adds up quickly.

My old trick was never to eat very much in one sitting. Instead, I
would eat little bits all through the day. Because it wouldn't make
me full, it didn't register that I was eating too much. For me, it
seemed like it hadn't happened. But by the end of the day, the
whole box of biscuits or the whole cake or whatever would have
disappeared! But how could it happen, I would wonder. I didn't
eat that much! That way I was sabotaging myself constantly.

Social sabotage

We are up against a lot trying to eat naturally. We are bombarded
with all kinds of adverts telling us to eat everything in sight, and yet
we are supposed to be sexy and slim. Because there is so much
thrown at us, we become accustomed to these messages and don't
even register them. And because there are so many conflicting
messages, we risk becoming unclear about who or what we are
trying to be. Who are we supposed to be as women: nurturers, food
preparers, mothers, sex symbols? Can we be all of these?

Life is about a primary need to feel lovable and to be able to
receive love. There is so much attention and pressure in our society
for women's figures to be a certain ideal. And this ideal determines
whether one is acceptable or lovable. Discrimination and social
unacceptability for being overweight abounds. It is no wonder that
millions of us put so much time and energy into altering our
bodies. It is not just a matter of being fashionable.

Being overweight or having a problem with eating has many
connotations. It means that we are lazy, self-indulgent and dull.
Worst of all, we are thought of as purposefully doing it to ourselves,
and it is only a matter of will-power that keeps us from having
great-looking bodies and controlling ourselves. It's odd, because
people who aren't very attractive facially tend not to be socially
acceptable either. But they aren't thought of as having caused their
own misfortune. Yet the overweight person, the compulsive eater,
is looked down upon, even though looks as well as body structure

are genetic creations. It is not only when we are adults that this type of attitude becomes noticeable. The stigma is perceived from a very young age. We learn to believe this for ourselves and we then pass these attitudes along to our own children. It comes as no surprise to me when a compulsive dieter tells me that his or her children are placing great importance on their body size or food. People try to be so perfect as parents, yet they manage to pass on all their neurotic tendencies, often without knowing it.

I was very sensitive to attitudes about weight from a very early age. I was even very sensitive to how clothes felt on my body as a small child. I can look at photos of myself in different outfits at different ages and remember what they felt like on my body. I was even conscious of whether I thought I looked fat in them or not. I would worry if clothes started to feel tight, almost as if it meant something 'awful' was about to happen. To this day, I can't stand to have anything tight around my waist because of the associations it has with being overweight. Even as a child, I would force myself into clothes that were tight so that I could identify with the smaller size, even though the tightness made me anxious.

In the United States, children's clothing is sized according to the age of the child. A five-year-old would probably need a size 5, for example, and I knew that. During one of our shopping expeditions, my mother picked out a size 6X dress for me. At the time I was six, so I thought I should still be getting a size 6. Obviously she knew something that I hadn't quite realised: 6 X was a size for chubby children. Manufacturers were beginning to produce a range of sizing for the overweight child. Without talking about it at all, I knew that wearing 6X meant I was entering into a whole new reality – the world where the pathetic overweight shopped. I felt I had passed a point of no return. I distinctly remember feeling that I wasn't normal because I had to choose this specially marked larger size. What made it worse was that I often had to order my clothes from a catalogue because not very many stores carried these new sizes. It created some anxiety to wait for the order to arrive in case it didn't fit. It seemed that everything about my weight produced some type of anxiety or self-consciousness. I focused a lot of attention on my body and what shape it was.

One day, my mother dropped my sister and me off at the hairdressers. My sister was about sixteen and I was seven. My mother had given the beauticians instructions to give us both perms. I had no desire to have one of those curly hair dos, nor did I want my hair cut off. I loved my long hair. When we got home, I went directly to a mirror where I could have a private look at the damage. I mourned the loss of my tresses and felt completely humiliated that I was to look like Little Orphan Annie until this ghastly curliness went away. I noticed how round it made my face look. I was already feeling quite round. I knew there was no way that I looked like a 'regular kid'. All I could feel was how it made me look fat. It was another incident that made me feel inferior and separate. And this made me want to eat.

I began comparing myself with others. I was looking at a photo of myself with the daughter of one of my mum's friends. She was about eight at the time. We were both dressed alike. I don't recall why we were in the same dresses, but we were. She was an 'ordinary size'. Even though she was two years older than me, I recall comparing my body to hers. It wasn't in the way you would expect. I wasn't thinking, 'Oh, look at how much taller she is' or 'look at her blonde hair'. I was looking at the photo in terms of proportions. 'She seems to be "normal-looking" but I look podgy. Am I going to get slimmer like her?' I always wondered what it felt like not to worry about one's body. I was sure that it must be very freeing not to have to take notice of yourself all the time. Sometimes I would think that I needed to find a way to alter my body. But I didn't see dieting as something I should do or even wanted to do, even though I knew I was overweight. I just wanted to eat and play and do the things kids do. I just wanted to eat the way other kids ate.

The media and fashion industries contribute much to unhealthy, competitive social standards. But every person who accepts and believes that these are true is also giving a message to the young that carries them into the next generation. It is as much down to those of us who allow ourselves to be discriminated against that these myths are perpetuated as it is to the nameless advertising empires that we attribute with creating them.

Much fashion advertising focuses on the smaller-than-average 'waif look', like fashion dummies, which basically have the bodies of pre-pubescent little girls. No hips, no breasts, no curves. How on earth are mature women supposed to regain that type of body once they have already gone into adulthood and possibly even had children? It is impossible, unless one becomes anorexic. So we have to ask ourselves, 'Why do we let this type of image set standards for grown-up women? Why should we feel bad about ourselves if we don't look like little boys?'

To be fair, the 'waif look' is not the only yardstick that we have to measure our bodies by. But you can be sure that the alternatives are still much smaller than the general population. Forty-seven per cent of British women are size 16 or above. Yet the other half of that population is defining our appearance. We must take stock and stand up for ourselves. Women should not feel so powerless in the market place when we are the ones who spend most of the money there. Women spend billions each year on clothing and make-up. Not to mention the other billions on weight-reducing schemes and products. We must see ourselves as consumers who make a difference. You *can* do something about the unrealistic standards that are shoved down your throat. You *can* do something about not having decent, fashionable clothes to choose from. And you don't have to carry a banner or get on national television to be taken notice of. You don't have to become a radical of this or that kind. But you can make an impact. You can spend your money in stores that cater for larger sizes. You can write letters to store managers saying why you are or are not shopping at their store. Actually, the industry doesn't care what it produces, it's only interested in demand and profit. If they see you as a profitable voice in the market place, they will respond. They'd love to make as much money from you as possible. Money talks. So let your money talk.

I don't mean to get into any political or feminist argument here. If you want to make feminist connections with your weight, then read Susie Orbach's *Fat Is a Feminist Issue*. This is certainly not my main focus. My point is that we are helping to perpetuate the 'body beautiful' myth by not demanding what we need and want. And I know it is very difficult to do this if you don't have very high self-esteem. Later in the course, we will discuss self-esteem in more detail. You are being conditioned every day to be discontent with your body, and you need to become very aware of the messages that are shaping your image about yourself and your worth.

THE INFLUENCE OF ADVERTISING

It is good practice to observe the messages that you get from adverts and television. We often don't even question them because we are so used to seeing them, but they do have quite a lasting effect on how we feel about ourselves. Subtly, every day, the messages are received and locked away in our subconscious. And if we are comparing ourselves to something unrealistic, we will only be building up more and more dislike for ourselves. This will not help you to come to peace with your body or with eating.

What do adverts tell us about ourselves as women? There are so many confusing images. Obviously we are supposed to be pleasing to look at and that means thin as well. Well, what if you're not? Does that mean you are not valued at all? I recently saw the results of a survey that showed how women's bodies have altered over the last forty years. The clothing measurements of the 1950s do not match up with the modern woman. The modern woman of the 1990s is definitely larger and has more fatty deposits. The hourglass figure is becoming a thing of the past. The classic 36–24–36 figure no longer applies – it is more like 37½–27–36 Our torsos are longer and our bottoms flatter. We are two inches taller, our arms are fleshier, our waist, neck, shoulders, abdomens and upper thighs have broadened two inches as well. Yet the 'ideal figure' that we are all striving for doesn't fit this description at all! It is totally unrealistic. Only a very small percentage of people naturally have the bodies that we are all trying to emulate.

CONFLICTING MESSAGES

Do you ever feel caught between double messages about food and eating? Do some people try to get you to eat and others admonish you for doing so? Do you suspect someone of trying to sabotage your efforts?

Lesley's mother demonstrated just such tactics. Whenever she fancied a snack or wanted to eat something 'bad', she would try to persuade Lesley to eat it with her at the same time. It confused Lesley, because most of the time her mother was trying to get her to diet. It always came as a surprise that her mother would offer her these things, because perhaps only an hour later she would see Lesley eating something and she would say, 'I thought you were on a diet, why are you eating that?' Her mother made her feel like a tennis ball being volleyed back and forth. She never knew if it was all right to eat or not. Lesley didn't realise at the time that her mother was not necessarily trying to sabotage her dieting with the snack offers, but that it was really her mother's own worries and guilt about eating that led to the double messages. For quite a while Lesley felt that her mother was purposely sabotaging her efforts.

Sometimes people will unconsciously try to undermine what you are doing. They are not necessarily doing it to hurt you, they are doing it to keep things stable. They don't want change, even if it might be for the best. People like to count on some type of familiarity and regularity in their relationships, and change can be very threatening, even if you are changing for the better. Change upsets the regularity that the ego is trying to preserve. This is one reason that you must take your loved ones through this process with you! That way they don't have to feel threatened and then they won't sabotage your work. You constantly need to talk about your feelings with your partner or your family and let them share their feelings, fears and hopes as well.

Catherine was suspicious of her husband's attitudes and behaviours in relation to her weight. Whenever she indicated that she hated her weight and was embarking on a new diet, he would seem to agree that she should do this and that he was supportive of her doing so. Sometimes he would even drive her to her slimming club meetings. As she started to lose some weight, he would seem pleased and even occasionally bring her a reward for doing so well. She thought it was curious, because sometimes his surprises were in the form of trinkets or flowers, but mostly they were some lovely,

45

gooey pastry which was definitely on her 'forbidden food' list. It was hard to resist when he brought these delights home, because she felt that she did deserve a reward for all her efforts. Her constant feelings of deprivation weakened her resolve, and she would find herself eating the treats and then feeling completely guilty. She would admonish herself and start again. It became a pattern for both of them. She would lose some weight, he would reward her, she would gain some weight back and then return to her diet. With so much toing and froing, she never seemed to gain any real ground. Her weight was essentially staying the same. After noticing this pattern, she began to express her disappointment and frustration with her husband. She discovered after a number of heart-to-hearts with him that he was sabotaging her weight loss. He wasn't doing it on purpose and he wasn't really aware of his part in the sabotage. He was acting out unconscious fear. On the surface, he did want her to lose weight, because he knew that would make her happy. He also liked how attractive and vivacious she became when she started feeling better about her body. But there was a part of him that was afraid she might leave him if she got too attractive or if she felt better about herself, she might wonder what was keeping her with him. So her weight loss was actually a threat for him. They talked it all through, and Catherine convinced him that she wasn't looking for a new man, she was looking for some freedom from food.

Then, of course, there may be those few who are consciously trying to undermine you. These people are doing it out of their own sense of insecurity and jealousy. They don't want to see you doing better than them. They don't want you to look nicer or get more attention. I should imagine though, that the number of people you would have contact with in that category would be quite low. However, if you have someone in your circle who is doing this, you must ask yourself why you put up with such a person. Is this person your friend?

The unfortunate fact of modern evolution is that women (and men) are conditioned to compete with each other. We are not raised to empower each other. We are taught to do better than our fellow man or woman. Someone must come out ahead. Being at the top, being the cream of the crop, gives you many advantages, from job possibilities to marital eligibility. And for women in particular, how you look makes a big difference in how you are received. So many women I speak to feel that they are distrustful of other women quite simply because they feel they are the opposition. This is not healthy, nor does it help advance people in relationships or promote any nurturing. And we are all in need of a great deal of nurturing, given our hectic and full lives. Remember that women are experts at nurturing. If you do not have any intimate friendships with women (by these I mean someone you really trust and can say anything to), then you are probably seriously under-nurtured.

Compulsive eating and weight have very little to do with food

The key to the problem is your attitude to yourself and your life. Your weight is largely dependent on your ability to receive and release. We receive and release in a variety of ways (I'm talking about receiving and releasing emotions and energy, as well as receiving and releasing food). This involves the whole body, not just what goes on in your head. Your body reflects your beliefs about life in general and how you see yourself. It demonstrates in a physical way what is going on emotionally and psychologically – it is actually your body's way of communicating with you. It also communicates a great deal to other people. Do you ever stop to listen?

YOUR BODY AS AN EMOTIONAL MIRROR

Have you ever noticed that when you are feeling good, you feel lighter? You are not quite able to pin-point exactly why, but weight just seems to disappear? And when things are not going smoothly or you are upset, the weight piles back on. But when you feel relaxed and at peace with yourself, you don't eat compulsively. This is no coincidence! Your body responds to you, because your body *is* you. One example of this occurs frequently when women fall in love. They seem automatically to lose weight. Often they will report continuing to eat the same amounts or perhaps even more! But this miracle weight-loss occurs in spite of all that. So what happens? Why is it so magical? Part of the answer lies in the fact that they have naturally taken their attention off their own negativity. They have dropped their problematic way of responding because they have been distracted by love. They forget to worry about their weight, so their body releases some of it. They stop blocking their energy. As they get happier, their body does too. We will examine this idea of losing weight through losing the preoccupation with self later.

ENERGY FLOW IN THE BODY

The body is energy and it conducts energy. If there are blocks in this circuit, you cannot possibly have balance with food or feelings. The body can easily get clogged up; we block this energy by holding onto emotions and suppressing them. We also block this energy with tension. You cannot possibly lose weight if you are fearful or full of tension. Nor can you lose weight if you are full of emotions. They are energy as well. You must learn to relax and breathe and let your body conduct the energy throughout its natural circuit. You have to relax to let the energy flow and release toxins in the form of oppressed feelings and weight. You cannot overeat if you are relaxed. It is impossible to be fully relaxed and overeat. The two don't match up. This is why learning to relax with your body and yourself and your eating is so very important. If you begin to relax and not worry about your weight or food, you will begin to see a difference in your weight stabilisation and your happiness.

When I was thirty-one, I thought that I was finished with my weight fluctuations forever. I had gone through being chubby as a kid, obese as a teenager, overweight as a young adult and anorexic just the year before. It had taken me four long years of rigorous dieting to become anorexic. I saw it as an accomplishment. But I had to really work at it. I weighed and measured my food every day. I ate the same things every day. Alcohol, sugar and starchy things never passed my lips. For most people, following this type of eating regime would have meant a large reduction in their size within a few months. But my weight came off extremely slowly.

Coming out of anorexia, my weight came back on slowly as well. It took me about two years to get back to my 'normal' weight. Even though I wasn't skinny any more, I also wasn't as obsessed with being thin. My eating behaviour had tamed considerably. Bingeing had ceased to be a problem, though sometimes I would overeat. But then, who doesn't?

So, here I was just trying to be normal about food, not making a big deal out of it one way or the other. However, I still knew I ate less than most other people. But at the same time, something began happening with my weight that I could not account for. I knew that I was gaining again. Only this time, it started happening very quickly. I was gaining at the rate of two to three pounds per week, and in five months, I had put on five stone! Of course, I looked immediately at my diet. Breakfast was now usually a bran muffin and an apple, lunch was an egg-salad sandwich and a cup of coffee and dinner was usually a salad or vegetable with some cheese on top. Occasionally, I would have a snack at night of a few crackers or rice cakes with a little honey or butter on. But these were not amounts of food that should be putting weight on anyone! It seemed completely ridiculous. I was not overeating, nor was I bingeing.

My roommate talked me into going to a naturopathic doctor. I had been to so many allopathic (conventional) doctors over the years who were completely uneducated about weight problems that I wasn't going to put myself through any more of that. But try as they might, the new doctors were not able to understand what was producing this enormous gain either. They tried me on some homeopathic remedies. At first it seemed they might have some effect, but I felt that something was blocking their healing potential. It took quite a while for me to realise that the blockage came from feelings about myself and my life.

I started to panic and to feel quite humiliated. I was hoping no one would notice how large I was getting, but I worked in an eating disorders programme – who on earth would have more attention paid to weight than the staff and patients in a programme like that! Everyone there thought that I had gone off the rails. They all thought I must be bingeing regularly to get so big so fast. I tried to tell people that I honestly wasn't, but even my best friend had doubt written all over her face. The more I was afraid I would gain weight, the more weight I would gain!

For a person who had just been successful losing weight, this was too much to bear. It was hard enough to accept that I wasn't skinny any more, but now I was becoming really obese! I felt I was being tortured. Every day my clothes got tighter and tighter. The more uncomfortable I was in my clothes, the more my attention was drawn to my body and how it felt. Mine felt terrible. I was becoming short of breath easily. I had little energy. I could feel the weight slowly building up around my limbs and torso. It was becoming harder and harder just to move through space. Jogging was now out because it hurt to have the fat jiggle up and down. Getting a massage was now out because my skin was so tight with the fullness that it hurt to touch it. Walking was difficult unless I was wearing trousers because my legs would rub together at the thighs, and my skin would chafe. I felt like a big blob. I didn't want to do anything physical. I didn't want to be in this body any more. It was too uncomfortable.

The physical discomfort was one thing, but the mental turmoil that this weight gain produced was worse than anything I had experienced in the past. I felt completely baffled. Nothing made sense anymore. Input did not equal output. There was no logical explanation and seemingly no physical condition to warrant these results. I felt ignorant and devastated. Here I was having spent most of my life figuring out weight control and now I was in this terrible position. I was suicidal and I wasn't just casually considering it. I had been going over in my mind how I would actually do it. I did not want to live in my body any more. There was just too much discomfort. I thought, if my best efforts got me to this point, what else is there? Even in the midst of not knowing why I had gained so much weight, I knew that dieting couldn't be an option any more, but I wasn't sure what else to do. I decided to go on an initial fast to lose some weight quickly, to get my spirits up. I went on a juice fast for one week. I took in only fruit and vegetable juices and tea. I had also consulted an **iridologist**, and she gave me a number of herbs to take daily for all the things she said were wrong with my health. For the next five weeks, I ate initially every fourth day, then every third day, then every second day until I was down at the last week to eating every other day. When I ate meals they were very light. Just a bit of fruit or veg. At the end of this six-week discipline, I found that I had lost no weight at all. I couldn't believe it. I thought it must be impossible.

Well, that was it for me. I thought, 'Forget it. I am never going to diet or alter my food again to try and lose weight.' I have stuck to this vow since 1985. I decided that I couldn't spend another moment focused on weight or restricting my food. I just didn't have the energy any more to consider new ways of trying to be thin. I conceded. The battle was over and my body had won. I gave up dieting altogether and just began eating whatever I wanted, whenever I wanted. If I wanted to eat chips and ice-cream for dinner, I did. If I didn't want to eat any vegetables or salad, I didn't. I figured I had already eaten enough salads in my life for at least three people! I realised that I had to associate with food in a much different way than I had before. All the taboos had to go. There were no longer 'good' foods or 'bad' foods. Food was just food, with no value or moral judgements to be placed on it. I also had to work to rid myself of the 'deprivation mentality' trap. If you're fat, you can't be seen to eat 'fun foods' or high-calorie foods. Nothing was out of bounds. And to my surprise, I didn't go out of control. I was afraid at first that if I let myself eat anything, then I would go wild and eat more and more. But instead what happened was that I no longer had any reason to worry about what I was going to have because I knew I could have anything whenever I liked. What a relief! I started to receive the food I was eating and to release the anxiety that I had built up. I noticed that my attention began to move away from food because I wasn't worried about it any more. I wasn't afraid that I would eat too much. I wasn't worried that it would make me gain weight. (After all, if I could gain so much weight without overeating, there *wasn't any point in beating myself up for eating normally.) I didn't think I had anything to lose. I was already at the most disgusting point I had ever been.*

For the first time in my life, I simply began to let my body tell me what to eat and when. Again, to my surprise I found that my body really did want to communicate with me. My body didn't like being overweight any more than the rest of me! I also stopped weighing myself. I just didn't see the point in it any more. I was huge and I didn't need a metal box to tell me so. I knew that I had to accept myself where I was and not live in the past or the future. I also had to accept that I might never be any other weight than I was then, which peaked at fourteen and a half stone.

An interesting thing happened at this point. Here I was, the fattest I had ever been. The most disgusting-looking, I thought. And yet I began to feel more like a woman. I began noticing how round and full my body was. It felt very nurturing in one aspect. I had never wanted to have curves or breasts, I had only ever wanted to be smooth with no bulges from anywhere! I let myself explore the possibility that fullness can be feminine.

I was beginning to experience a sense of freedom that I hadn't had before. I was beginning to become involved in life, rather than just conscious about what my body looked like at any given time. I noticed how much time and attention I had for many other interests and relationships. I was amazed how much time and energy I had devoted to the pursuit of being thin. And the pursuit never made me happy, not even when I was skinny. The pursuit never even made sense. The amount of weight I lost didn't correlate with the amount I starved myself. And the same went for the opposite end of the spectrum. The amount of food that I ate had no logical bearing on the rapid weight gain I experienced. It was clear to me that my weight had very little to do with what I had eaten.

FREE YOURSELF!

Concentrate on what you are not accepting and begin to liberate yourself from your bondage. You need to give your body a break. Let it get on with things naturally and stop overriding yourself physically. Take your eyes off your thighs and get in touch with what is going on inside you instead. Let yourself start the process of learning to receive and release.

There are a number of ways you can begin to emancipate yourself. No matter what you think about yourself, you must allow others to give energy to you. This can take many forms. It can be by allowing someone to do you a favour, to help you out in some way. Let people have the opportunity and the pleasure of doing something for you. You do not have to be eternally grateful to them. You do not have to try to reciprocate in kind. You are practising receiving. Often people think that it is selfish to receive, but receiving is not the same thing as being self-centred! Some people think that if they allow themselves to receive, then they will only be takers in life or they will become lazy. I can guarantee from knowing the type of person that you are that this will not be the case, because you are not very proficient at receiving. You need training in this area. You need to practise receiving without feeling that you have to do something about it.

One area in which we are poor receivers is with our food. Swallowing food faster than we can register it is not receiving! Feeling guilty about what we are eating, or feeling that we have to conceal what we have eaten is not a gesture of welcoming the life force that the food contains. This only produces tension, and tension produces energy blockages. If you do not feel it is appropriate to enjoy the food that you eat, then you are not accepting it into your body. It is not likely to get processed properly and may accumulate as waste. You are creating an energy block with that food.

Allow yourself to receive emotional support from others. Improve relationships with those close to you. If they tell you that they love you, there is no reason you should doubt this. If they tell you that you look nice, you must believe they are telling the truth. How do you feel when you pay someone a compliment and they brush it off? You can feel that they are not willing to receive from you. How does this make you feel? You desperately need to learn to accept love from others and from yourself.

Let yourself be free. Free from the demand to be anything other than who you are. There is absolutely nothing the matter with you.

You are a human being and by that very fact you deserve love and respect. Allow yourself to examine what changes *you* want to make in your life. Drop the enormous expectations that you have about weight. Your body will help you put your weight back into place.

HOMEWORK

PRACTICAL STEPS

- Have a look in your wardrobe. Are you keeping clothes that are too tight in the hopes that one day you will get back into them? Throw out, give away or at least pack away the clothes that do not fit you today. You are subtly torturing yourself by keeping them. Don't wear anything that makes you feel fat or frumpy. Don't wear clothes that are too tight. Buy yourself at least a few things that you can feel good in. This does not mean that you have to spend a lot of money on clothing, nor does it mean that you have resigned yourself to being a size you don't like. But you must begin to live in the present. This is the size you are today, so accept it. Try to be as comfortable in your clothes as you can so that your attention is not always going to your body and what's wrong with it. (See the Resources section for clothing stores that cater for larger sizes.)

- You are in the process of retraining yourself to eat freely and without guilt, but it doesn't serve your purpose to keep foods around that you know you will think about until you have eaten them all. This works against you. If there is something that you want to eat that is a difficult food to stay away from, then make a point of going out and buying just one of it; take it home or eat it out and let yourself completely enjoy it. Then you can relax, knowing that you don't have to think about it any more. You can eat whatever you want whenever you want if you are really hungry, but you also need to be smart about how you do it. Don't torture yourself!

WRITTEN EXERCISES

1 Why is your weight important to you? What do you hope to change about

55

your life if you change your weight?

2 How do you feel about yourself? Are you acceptable with your family, friends, social circles?

3 Are there any people who sabotage your progress? How do they attempt to do that? Have you spoken to them about it?

4 Do you think you have a realistic idea about how much you actually eat each day?

5 Are there certain foods that you avoid? Do you have a 'forbidden' or 'bad' food list? What's on it?

6 Do you allow yourself to receive love and affection from others? Can you take a compliment gracefully? Do you feel loved? Do you feel desired?

7 What don't you want to accept about yourself? Why do you feel you are inadequate as you are?

5

chapter five

THOSE FOUNDATION YEARS

> ❧ *'An individual's sense of self and worth in our society is, partly at least, a socially and psychologically based phenomenon, and becomes established in relation to the social and cultural context, initially provided by the family and its value systems, beliefs and capacity to care and nurture.'* ❧

[From *Anorexia Nervosa: Let Me Be*, A.H. Crisp]

I know this may seem like a very dry, 'Freudian' chapter, but bear with me. It's actually going to be interesting because it's about you and your family.

The family, your family, no matter what you think of it, is very important. It plays a primary role in how you develop as a person and how you see yourself in relation to other people. Your relationship with your parents colours everything that you do in life. This begins at the very earliest of ages. Your basic personality is completely in place by the time you are just three years old!

We are shaped by the structure and beliefs that our parents provide for us. Genetically, you have been passed certain physical and personality characteristics. Emotionally, you have amassed a plethora of feelings about life. Your family was a mini-society, with its own governing system, politics, economics, culture and beliefs. How you operated within that structure is how you operate out in

57

the world. Therefore, two useful pieces of your puzzle are to look at what you cultivated from your family and how you interact with others. This will equip you with a picture of your basic belief system.

Family inheritance

There is no way of knowing at birth who will struggle with their weight or, for that matter, what will become of each person. It is usually after the fact that we go back and rediscover or uncover what it was that made us into the type of person we have become. We respond to our life circumstances according to how we view ourselves and people in general. Everything shapes us in our process of growing and changing, and nothing influences our initial development as much as the dynamic within our families. The emotional bond between parent and child is stronger than any other relationship that we will enter into in life. They are the most primary relationships that we have because they are our first introduction to human beings. We depend on them completely for all our needs and we must trust them implicitly for our very lives. What we feel about our parents and the interactions that we have with each other make lasting impressions on us emotionally. We have developed a whole pattern of relating and reacting to others in accordance with what we felt to be true as a child. That doesn't mean, however, that parents are completely responsible for making us the people that we become. We do have a part in it ourselves!

As children, we are not capable of intellectualising the information that we take in. We soak up emotional messages on a psychic level and then translate them into beliefs. Beliefs about ourselves, the world and other people. This is the reason why people feel scarred from certain events in their chilhood. Children don't have the capacity to sort things out logically – all they feel is the emotional data locked into place. As adults, we have the opportunity to take that emotional data and see if it still fits. We can decide what is old and useless and what is true in the present.

BELIEF SYSTEMS ARE ARBITRARY!

People act as though their beliefs are set in stone and cannot be changed. This just simply is not true. Beliefs are learned and they can be unlearned or relearned. People generally decide what it is they believe very early on in life. What you believe is based on what you were taught or what your parents believe. Most people raised in a particular religion or political system tend to continue to adhere to those beliefs as adults. And this even extends to the types of food that you eat. If you ate something as a child, you will most likely continue to eat it as an adult. Foods that you didn't like as a child, or wouldn't try, will most likely be foods that you still won't eat. How many of us have to have certain foods prepared the way our mothers made them?

Unfortunately, some people either never take the time or are too afraid to look at their belief systems. If they have experienced a trauma, it may just remain in place. Our responses are generally stuck in a repetitive, automatic pattern. We continue to put ourselves into situations that confirm our basic beliefs about life. This would be fine if our basic beliefs were positive and nurturing. But we generally put ourselves into situations that confirm that we are unloved. It takes a lot of courage to allow ourselves to examine past hurts. But the beauty of it is that, by exploring these, we can release useless emotional baggage and pain. We can then get on with our lives in a more expansive and nourishing way.

I cannot put too much emphasis on this area – it is vitally important. You have taken your beliefs and you use them every day. So if what you believe about yourself is negative, you are going to continue to reinforce that for yourself every day and in every way that you can.

From as far back as I can remember, I felt that there was something inherently the matter with me. This feeling goes back farther than my visual memory, even though I never had reason to doubt that my parents loved me and wanted me. And even though I felt that they did, I still had this uneasy feeling of being unacceptable. So I know that this feeling did not come from them, but from me.

*When I was about four years old or so, I was painfully shy around strangers. My mother said that I would often run and hide whenever we had company. I don't remember hiding, but I do remember feeling shy. I also had a habit of wrinkling up my nose when I was nervous. I must have looked rather like a bunny rabbit! I was completely aware that I did this, but I wasn't able to stop doing it. It would happen without thinking. My parents procured some pills from our family GP that apparently were to help me with my shyness and nervous wrinkling. To this day, we don't know what exactly was in the pills, but my mother did say they made a marked change in my disposition. Perhaps they were tranquillisers or maybe even **placebos**. Who knows. For some reason, my father still had the tablets years later. I found them when I was in college; the label read 'For Genevieve Blais, 1 tablet per day for confidence'.*

At that age, I didn't think that wrinkling my nose or being shy was a problem. I only knew that mummy and daddy gave me some medicine to make me different. My memory of those tablets was not that they gave me confidence, but that there was something the matter with my personality that needed to be altered. This was the emotional data I was storing away. I'm sure my parents were only trying to help me get through this shy phase. But for me, it confirmed that I wasn't all right as I was. And that essentially became my basic premise in life. I spent many, many years trying to figure out how I should look and be.

Memory mapping

Let's do an exercise that will help to point out your tendencies, belief systems and patterns. You are going to map out a chronological history of yourself. Don't worry if you don't have a lot of childhood memories to go by, this exercise will help stimulate memories that you can write in at a later date It is also not important if what you remember is technically accurate or not. What is important about memory is what emotions you were left with about a certain incident or relationship.

Make a chart and mark down any major events in your life, starting as far back as you can remember. You can also include events that you were told about but may not have any memory of yourself. These can be any moves that you made, like moving house or changing schools, or they can be anything that you considered to be big or traumatic events, like births, deaths, marriages, etc. Then mark down what age you were when it occurred and what weight you were. (If you can't remember accurately, just estimate or say, 'I was chubby' or 'a teenager', etc.) The last piece of information you put alongside the others is your dominant emotion linked with this incident: 'I was very angry or sorrowful' or 'I hated my mum', etc. Below is a sample of what your chart will look like. Take it as far as you can, including your recent past. This will give you a good look at the patterns in your life.

SAMPLE CHART

age 3	age 9	age 11
weight — a little chunky	weight — a little chunky	weight — about a stone overweight
incident — dog run over	incident — sister in accident	incident — mum put me on diet pills
feeling — sad and angry, betrayed by mother	feeling — sorry for sister, scared fearful of father	feeling — didn't want to diet, wanted mother to back off

When I was about three or four years old, there was an incident that is engraved in my memory forever. I didn't even remember this event until I was in my early thirties. One weekend, whilst participating in a self-improvement seminar, a visualisation came flooding into my consciousness. Within a few seconds, I realised why I had always had a strained relationship with my mother. It revolved completely around one interaction.

We had a new puppy named Buttons. One day, while he and I were out playing in our garden, he managed to find a hole in the fence and climb through it. He bounced off down the driveway and into the busy street in front of our house. As you can imagine, a street with heavy traffic was no match for this little creature. Unfortunately I was trying to locate him when I saw him get run over by a passing car. I was shocked and devastated.

I went running into the house to find my mother and tell her of this horror. I will never quite know the accuracy of what I remembered about what happened next because it's coloured by my emotional response to the trauma. My memory is that my mother had a woman over for tea at the time. When I went to deliver the horrible news, I was met with the response, 'Not now, we have company, I'll handle this later.' I couldn't believe the coolness and lack of compassion and empathy. (It does seem odd, because my mother is actually fairly highly strung. Her usual response to upsets was to get a bit hysterical.) Whatever her actual response was, my heart was broken. I was in a state of shock and didn't know what to do with myself. Everything was in a whirl. I don't even remember what happened next, whether the woman left or we went outside to get my puppy, nothing. I only remember feeling completely betrayed by my mother at the time.

As an adult, I realised that when this memory came to the forefront, I had made some major life decisions that day. My first response was, 'Well, forget you, if you are my mother and you don't want to take the time to console me over this great loss, then I don't love you and I'm not going to let you get close to me. You don't fit my idea of a mother.' This was the beginning of shutting my mother out of my life. I'm sure she felt my withdrawal in many ways. But I had decided that she couldn't be trusted with my feelings; and if she wasn't trustworthy, then other women weren't either. A sort of 'if A equals B and B equals C, then A equals C' mentality. It is unfortunate that I cut myself off emotionally from my mother, because it meant that I wasn't able to receive the nurturing that she wanted to give me at other times.

My second reaction was that if something this traumatic had occurred and there was so little response, then it must mean that my feelings weren't important. I realised that I would have to begin expressing myself in a much more dramatic way to make people pay attention to me. I took all of these feelings and presumptions into adulthood with me, as we all do.

This difficult pattern emerged in my relationship with my mother early on. I felt betrayed by her and did not trust her. I didn't want to give her any energy, because I wanted to punish her for not being the mother I wanted her to be. I wanted her just to leave me alone. And because of how I felt about her, I didn't trust other women or feel that I wanted to get close to them either. I looked to my father for any approval I wanted.

A second very influential event for me happened when I was nine. My sister was about eighteen at the time and had a boyfriend that my father didn't particularly like. She wanted to go and visit him one night, but knew that he would say no. So she lied and told him that she was going to go and do an errand for him and took off in the family car (her boyfriend lived out in the country). On her way out there, she missed a curve in the road. The car went down a sixty-foot embankment and landed on the driver's side. Luckily, she got thrown out on the way down or she would have been killed. But she was pretty badly hurt and had to claw her way up the hill with slivers of glass embedded in many parts of her body. She had lost her two front teeth from the impact. I remember being very shocked when I saw her in hospital. She looked so frail and vulnerable, and I wondered if she would die. She was a horrific sight.

My father was so angry with her for lying to him that he told her he was disowning her. When she had recovered from her injuries, he gave her some money and kicked her out of the house. My mother and my brothers and I drove her to the YWCA to live. It was a very sad incident. She never lived with us again.

I didn't realise at the time just how emotional this event was for me, partly because I would never allow myself to think poorly of my father. I thought it was because I admired him so much. But later I realised that it was probably more out of fear. If I didn't want to be close to my mother and if I pulled away from my father, then I wouldn't have anyone! I also knew that if he could do that to my sister when she was in such a vulnerable state, then he might find a reason to cut me out of his life as well.

This added to my feeling that life was very precarious. People might appear trustworthy on the surface, but you had to be very careful not to get crushed. It seemed that being vulnerable was too risky. I learned how to put on a coat of armour against the world. I now had to protect myself against my father as well.

What I felt about my father emerged much later in life for me. Since I withdrew from my mother at an early age, I aligned myself to my father. As he was the one with the power in the family, it was necessary for me to avoid feeling anything negative about him. In my late thirties I realised that my relationship with my father had actually coloured my belief system much more than my relationship with my mother. I noticed that my basic beliefs in life were: 1) Women are not valued as much as men and can never be worth as much simply because of their gender; 2) Do not trust people with your feelings – handle them yourself; 3) Being vulnerable is a very risky business; 4) Men run the world and one must please them to survive. I also felt a strong need to compete with men to prove my competence.

Given these kinds of beliefs, you can imagine the type of life I created for myself so that I could confirm that what I believed was true. I competed with my brothers for good grades and degrees. I became an over-achiever to prove that I was competent. I put myself in situations where I was working with men so that I could gain their acceptance and attention. I didn't have much use for women because I distrusted them and considered that I was in competition with them for the attention of men.

One of my good friends, Jerri, has a very interesting emotional memory from when she was six months old. Her mother was pregnant with her sister at the time and was having a very difficult pregnancy with a lot of morning sickness. You can imagine having to take care of an infant while being ill with another one on the way. Jerri actually remembers that sometimes when her mother was feeding her or holding her, she would have to get up and go to be sick. She would put Jerri down quickly and dash off. Jerri's emotional perceptions from that time are that she literally made people sick and she had to be thrown away!

Often people will uncover very early or even **pre-verbal** memories like this. You don't have to remember a specific incident either to remember an emotional memory.

> *A client of mine named Shelly was trying to discover why she has always felt inadequate. What she realised from doing this exercise was that her parents wanted and expected her to be a boy. They didn't even have a girl's name chosen. They had decided they were having a boy! This feeling was strengthened because her father treated her as if she was a boy. He wanted to do male types of things with her, teach her to fish and box and play football. Shelly, though, just wanted to be a girl. So she constantly felt she was a disappointment. Failing at weight control is a very good way for her to reinforce that she is a disappointment.*

The point of the exercise is to start showing you what you believe about yourself and life in general. It will also point out similarities between your eating and your emotional states. We establish early on what we feel our 'script' is and then spend the rest of our lives playing it out. We tend to put ourselves in situations where the outcome will confirm what we already believe. We choose our friends and spouses for the same unconscious reasons. You can see, therefore, that it is a good idea to examine what we believe so we can make conscious choices in life rather than wonder why we keep repeating the same painful experiences.

Give yourself a lot of time to do this exercise. You may want to do it in pieces, a little bit every day. It is good just to keep adding to it. You may be surprised at how many things comes to mind once you get started! Ask yourself these questions after completing this exercise:

- Did you notice any patterns with regards to prominent feelings or weight changes?
- Can you begin to see what you believe about yourself and life?
- Are the things that you presume about yourself true?

Now fill in the blanks in the following section. This will help show you the conclusions that you have come to.

Life Beliefs

Life is _____ .

I am _____ .

The most important thing to me in life is _____ .

I want _____ .

I can get what I want by _____ .

We need to begin making choices rather than riding on our automatic reactions or continuing to believe what we were told because we haven't taken the time to examine our lives. Often, I work with women who haven't got a clue what it is they want or need because they have never taken the time to examine anything. They just presume that they have to take what life hands them, especially if they already feel inferior because of their weight.

How we get our ideas

We learn who we are and what we believe through a number of different sources. The first, as I have stated, is our parents. We also learn from our peers, our relatives, advertising, books, radio and television.

A lot of our learning has to do with the verbal mind. We learn through words, spoken or written. We take these words and turn them into concepts. We take these concepts and live our lives according to them. We repeat these actions, often without even questioning where their motivation came from in the first place.

Sometimes even one phrase deposited at a vulnerable moment can remain with a person the whole of their life. And worse, it can distort a person's self-perception throughout their life. Here are a few examples of seemingly innocuous remarks that had long-lasting effects on the people who received them.

Claudia, a woman of seventy-one who came to me for help with her weight, said that one of her biggest problems was that she was and had always been extremely self-conscious. She was very timid about making any decisions and quite nervous at the idea of trying anything new. When we talked about her upbringing, I discovered that she was raised by her older sister. This sister remarked to her when she was young, 'You nearly killed your mother when you were born.' This statement has never left her. Is it any wonder that Claudia has always felt tenuous about her own existence? She practically murdered the one who gave her life and who then wouldn't even raise her! She learned to tread softly and not to trust herself or her actions. Claudia has carried this negativity about herself for over sixty years!

Unwitting remarks do not necessarily have to be overtly about food or one's body to have an impact on a person's eating behaviour.

Sandra, age thirty-five, cannot remember ever feeling as if she belonged in her family. She used to think maybe she was adopted, although she wasn't. She was never able to reconcile how it was that she ended up living with these strangers. She didn't share any of their beliefs about life, yet she took some of them on board regardless. Her parents were very restrained emotionally. Neither of them showed their feelings. They were working class and didn't like this position in life. But they felt powerless to change their position because of what they believed, not because of the lack of opportunity. They were unhappy about life and felt trapped. Sandra, on the other hand, is a very demonstrative, cuddly, light-hearted person. She has always maintained that there is a lot of life to be lived and she wants to be part of it all. She likes people who are open and adventurous. She is creative with her children and has had numerous promotions in her work. And yet there is one simple phrase that her father would utter over and over that keeps her suspended from realising her potential. Whenever anyone in the family aspired to anything, no matter how humble or insignificant, he would say, 'People like us don't do that.' To this day, Sandra has difficulty in feeling that she has the right to have accumulated anything nice for herself or her family. She feels she shouldn't assert herself in any significant or successful way because it would be out of place. She has passed up job offers so she wouldn't appear ambitious. And deep down, she doesn't believe that she can be anything but fat because that is her lot in life.

Here's one that just broke my heart.

Rosemary actually felt that she would be doing her daughter a favour by calling her derogatory names that had to do with her weight. Her thinking was: because her daughter was overweight, she was bound to be teased, so if she teased her at home, she would get used to the ridicule and not be sensitive to it when others did it to her. I had a great deal of difficulty listening to that one. My heart was bleeding for this young girl. How could anyone think that humiliating someone could have any positive effect?

Here is a sample of some other one-liners that have set people back.

- *'A good mother feeds her children lots of food.'*
- *'Can't you do anything right?'*
- *'You will never amount to anything.'*
- *'Can't you behave like your sister?'*

NON-VERBAL INFLUENCE

We learn not only from verbal messages but from non-verbal messages as well. You don't have to be told something in order to take it into your belief system. In fact, non-verbal messages can be even more potent than verbal ones. The old adage 'actions speak louder than words' is very true. Children as well as adults pick up things on a **psychic** or 'feeling' level from others. Children are like little psychic sponges. When you are a child, you are constantly watching others and imitating them. Watching others is one way that we develop our own patterns of behaviour. For instance, if a child never sees his parents cuddling or being affectionate, then he will think that it is not an appropriate behaviour. Whether or not the child might like to be demonstrative, he will tend to suppress being that way because he doesn't think it's 'normal'. We develop all kinds of attitudes by watching what our parents do.

An area that influences our beliefs and actions a great deal is our sexuality. What we see our parents demonstrate in this area affects our attitudes about ourselves and our own sexuality. If your parents were pretty 'buttoned down' in terms of talking about themselves as sexual beings, you will feel that somehow it is wrong or not appropriate to talk about it. It works with every area of our lives. We tend to see the world from much the same perspective as our parents, and we are inclined to have very similar lifestyles to them. There isn't anything wrong with this, but if you have developed patterns of behaviour or beliefs that you don't like but feel stuck with, then you need to examine them. The mere fact that you are reading this indicates that your way of coping is, to some degree, not working for you any more.

MEDIA STEREOTYPES

We are also quite influenced by the media and other people. What kinds of messages do you believe to be true about fat people or thin people? The general public would lead you to believe that over-weight people are stupid, lazy, self-indulgent, ugly, unappealing, undeserving of love or affection, and not as good as others. Thin people, on the other hand, are thought to be happy, have their lives sorted out, be sexy, smart, appealing, and can have or eat whatever they want. The problem is that we believe these attitudes and feel bad about ourselves because of them.

What do people tell you about yourself? Do you just believe it because you think your feelings don't matter because of your weight or what you look like?

- What do you believe about yourself?
- How do you see yourself?

- How do you want to see yourself?
- How do you see yourself in the future?

Positive mental attitude

The influence of a person's mental attitude should not be under-estimated. The mind is a very powerful thing, so you should use it to your advantage and stop acting as though it has control over you. In fact, your mind is the only thing in life that you *do* have control over. You can programme in or delete any information that you wish. You can create or stop any thought that you like. You must take charge of your mind because it is not particularly discriminative on your behalf. It does not care whether or not you are programming in negative or positive information. It simply takes the information that you've put in and continues to play it over and over again. (This happens mostly on an unconscious level.) So it is very important to programme it very carefully. Most people tend to lean towards feeding the mind negative information. Fear is one emotion that helps to hold weight on the body. Not because fear can do this in itself, but because it is a part of negativity. If you are afraid that you will gain weight, you will because that is what you are essentially programming in. It is what you expect to happen.

In any self-improvement, personal achievement or prosperity seminar that you might participate in, you will hear about the power of positive thinking. This is because it does make a huge difference to the outcome. People often believe that they really want positive things to happen, but on an unconscious level they are actually blocking the positive with old negative tapes. If what you really wanted was to be a certain weight, you would be. And if you're not, that means that something is blocking your achievement. You have a conflict going on somewhere. This doesn't mean that you aren't clever enough to have figured it out already. You just didn't know where to look for the information that could make a difference.

THE POWER OF AFFIRMATION

Giving yourself positive affirmations every day is one way to regain control over your mind and your destiny. You don't have to believe what you're saying initially. (And it is highly likely that you won't because you are so conditioned to think poorly of yourself.) But if you repeat affirmations to yourself every day, you will begin to adopt a different attitude towards yourself. Start with a good general one. Look in a mirror every day and say, 'Every day, in every way, I am getting better and better.' Or you can just repeat it to yourself silently. Do this for at least thirty days and you will begin to notice a difference in your outlook and your attitude. (It takes at least thirty days to change a pattern. Remember this when we talk about changing patterns in chapter 8.) Once you get used to addressing yourself in a more positive way, you will begin to like it and you will want to repeat it. When you feel more comfortable with affirmations, you may be able to move on to say something positive about your body!

DON'T TORTURE YOURSELF

Who you are is not the body. The body is part of how you manifest yourself in the world, but it is not the sum total of who you are. Your weight or your looks are not your worth. You have to get out of this type of thinking. The same goes with your response to scales and weighing yourself. You cannot let a little metal box determine whether or not you are a 'good' person or whether or not you should be happy. It is not helpful to weigh yourself a lot. It is much better to weigh yourself only about once a month. And always weigh yourself at the same time each month. If you start to do it in the middle of a month, then continue to weigh yourself in the middle of the next month. Weight is a very relative thing; our bodies are made up of a lot of fluid, so our weight fluctuates every day. This is the natural course of things! You are not getting a true reading if you are jumping on and off the scales every hour or every day. This is another way that you torture yourself and it is unnecessary. You must stop punishing yourself for not liking the size of your body.

HOMEWORK

PRACTICAL STEPS

- Begin to pay attention to what others are saying. Do you believe things that are negative about yourself? Are you letting the hype of advertising and magazines determine your value?

- You must begin to change your mental attitude about yourself. Start saying something positive about yourself every day. I know this seems corny, but it does work.

- Become a keen observer of what you are doing and what you are feeling.

- Continue to practise guilt-free eating.

- Start to notice your breathing patterns. How do you breathe? Do you breathe from the abdomen? Do you breathe when you eat or are you anxiously holding your breath?

WRITTEN EXERCISES

1 Write down any patterns that you noticed from your memory-mapping exercise. Were there any surprises for you?

2 How did you feel about your parents/siblings when you were growing up? How do you feel about them now? What was your parents' disposition towards you?

3 Who were you most aligned to? Did they ever betray you? Do you still feel betrayed by them?

4 What do you believe about life in general? Is it a happy existence? Unhappy?

5 Where do you fit into the scheme of things? What do you believe about yourself? Are you a 'good' person, etc.? Is it true? What do you *want* to believe about yourself?

6 Write the letter that you always wanted to give to your mother (whether she is still alive or not). List all the things that you ever wanted to say to her. (This letter

will not be sent anywhere, so you are free to say exactly what you feel.) After you have finished it, write a letter to yourself from your mother. How would she answer you?

7 Write the letter that you always wanted to give to your father. Do the same as in question 6 then write an answer to yourself from your father.

6

chapter six

EMOTIONAL ILLUSIONS – FEELINGS AND ATTITUDES

Weight and eating are emotional issues for most women because both are linked with self-esteem and virtue. This produces a serious dilemma for people who struggle with either or both of these. They feel terrible about themselves if they overeat compulsively or are overweight, and they expect others to chastise them for it. And whether they struggle with their weight or not, most people have an opinion about being overweight.

There are some careers (modelling, dancing, air hostessing, etc.) that put constant pressure on employees to remain a certain size. But it is not just the obvious careers where thinness is a requirement. This 'bodyism' permeates many conventional careers as well. I have heard countless stories of people going for jobs as receptionists or front-line secretaries or positions that involve greeting the public or hosting executives who were turned down because of their weight. Usually they were not told directly why they had been disqualified, but some were told they did not possess the 'image' that the company was looking for. Translated, that meant they wanted someone slender who could slink their way in a lycra mini skirt to the coffee machine. How many of us fit that description?

It is interesting that, in a recent article in *The Times* (10 April

74

1994), Mary Ann Sieghart (who is a size 10) wrote that even she thinks the 'ideal' woman's shape is impossible for all but a very few. With all the pressure on women to be thinner than what is natural or possible for most, she says, 'It's no surprise that women's esteem is low: that they feel fat even when they are not.' So we're not just talking about overweight people being damaged emotionally because of 'bodyism', but slender people as well.

And judgements are rampant everywhere. A vast number of people assume that if a person is overweight, they have consciously chosen to be so and it is only a lack of will-power or slovenliness that keeps them fat. On the other hand, if a person has cancer or some other debilitating disease or handicap, people tend to show them a great deal of compassion. They are not made to feel guilty because of their suffering! But people who are overweight are treated as if they did it to themselves simply by overeating and, if they would just control themselves by not putting so much food into their mouths, they could easily lose weight. For those of us who have ever struggled with our weight and have gone on every diet possible, we know that it is not just a matter of will-power or choosing to be fat or slim.

Claire and her husband decided it was time to start their family. She had the usual worries and doubts about becoming pregnant because she was already overweight. She felt that it wasn't acceptable for her even to want *to get pregnant because of her size. She felt it was not responsible. She worried about what others would think. She also feared she might not be able to lose the weight she gained in pregnancy. What should have been a very happy nine months of Claire's life was filled with doubts about herself as a person and as an expectant parent. One of her greatest torments were her monthly pre-natal check-ups. Of course, she was weighed before seeing the doctor. This caused her a great deal of anguish and anxiety. The nurse who weighed her always had a patronising comment to make to Claire about her weight. This made Claire feel she was doing something wrong. It made her feel ugly and accused. And it made her feel angry that she couldn't stand up to the woman because she felt so bad about herself. And after all, the nurse was right, she was overweight. Guilty as charged! Claire often stopped on the way home from these visits to get herself some binge foods to quash her feelings. This perpetuated her guilt and paranoia.*

It has been well noted in *Binge Eating* by Fairburn and Wilson that overeating is often preceded by feelings of failure and inadequacy. This in itself suggests that focusing only on food intake is targeting the wrong area when we are trying to help people with food compulsions. Instead of looking at a proposed lack of will-power, people should be looking at what it is that makes them feel distressed.

THE EFFECTS OF DISCRIMINATION

Discrimination has a very harmful emotional impact on human beings. If someone is large and receives negative responses because of their size, then they begin to feel more dissatisfaction with themselves. It makes people dissociate from their bodies even more. And it increases their feelings of inadequacy. The very people who need to have the most self-compassion turn against themselves. Overweight people are not just being paranoid. Your size makes a difference in this society as to how you are treated. If you want to go into detail about sizeism, you can read Shelley Bovey's book *Being Fat Is Not a Sin.* She has covered this topic in great detail.

We live in a society where body image denotes acceptance and worth. That, at least, is the case in our Western, 'thin-obsessed' cultures. It has not always been this way, nor is it the same everywhere. In the days of the cavemen and women, storing up extra weight could mean the difference between surviving the winter or not. In the earlier part of this century too, thin women were categorized as undesirable, unmarriageable, spinster types. Being thin also signified a type of personality that was rigid and without humour or warmth.

In India, with its long history of famine, being overweight is seen as a sign of wealth. In Africa, there are cultures who purposely fatten up their teenage daughters as part of preparing them for marriage. In the South Pacific, there are many cultures where large, round bodies are the norm for women as well as men. Being thin is the exception, not the rule.

Fat fallacies

As sensitive, impressionable people, we often take on opinions or ideology about our identities on a subconscious level, even though we may feel in our hearts that they are wrong. There are many myths or fallacies about weight and social standards that are simply rubbish. But we have been fed them for so long, we lose our ability to distinguish fact from emotional blackmail. Prejudice is another means to cajole people into conforming to a certain ideal, and if they won't conform, then we oppress them.

First, individuals need to decide where they are in relation to their weight. Would they mind being the size they are if there wasn't so much bias about it? Do they want to lose weight, or do they just want to be treated with respect? This makes all the difference in terms of procedure.

FAT FALLACY NO. 1

All fat people desire to be thinner.

FAT FALLACY NO. 2

Fat people can't be beautiful or sensual or sexual. Only thin people are sexy.

FAT FALLACY NO. 3

Fat people can't possibly be happy with themselves or their body. Only thin people are happy.

Actress and comedienne Dawn French, who also happens to be a large, voluptuous and beautiful woman, is completely happy with her weight. She does not fit the social idea of size at all, nor does she care to. When interviewed in *She* magazine (May 1994) she remarked that she has always been large and has never had any hang-ups about it, other than finding shopping for clothes difficult. Her process has not been to try and shrink herself to fit, but to speak out for herself and for others who are happy with their bodies. Ms French has been using her high profile to quash the fallacy that large women are non-sexual, non-sensual beings. She is a walking advertisement of the attractiveness of ample flesh. She has even opened a clothing store in London called '1647' to provide quality clothing for the forty-seven per cent of the female population that are size 16 and over. And she works in collaboration with designer Helen Teague to create beautiful clothes that make big women feel beautiful. That seems to me to be a very positive use of her energies.

On the other hand, the overweight men clients I have had don't have nearly the same emotional trauma associated with their weight as my women clients. It's not that they *like* being overweight, but it's had little bearing on their feelings of manliness or power or acceptability in society. Many of my male clients' reasons for wanting to lose weight have to do with building physical stamina and increasing their feelings of well-being. Whereas for women, it is often to develop a sense of self!

FAT FALLACY NO. 4

Fat people are unhealthy. If you are thin, it means that you are physically fit.

There is a lot of confusing information about health around. How do you decide who to believe? It used to be a commonly held truth that being fat made one unhealthy and at risk from numerous diseases and early death, including heart disease, hypertension, high blood pressure, diabetes, gall bladder trouble and even certain cancers. More recent research (by Garner and Garfinkel, 1985) is proving this idea incorrect. It is showing that there is little evidence to prove that being overweight increases the risk of physical maladies. If someone is obese and they develop a disease, then their weight will magnify the condition, but it does not mean that it created it. And, in fact, the enormous amount of pressure put on people to lose weight and the stress associated with dieting can be enough to produce poor health! In many cultures where obesity is high but is the social norm, the frequency of heart disease and diabetes is lower than in cultures where it is unacceptable.

FAT FALLACY NO. 5

Only fat people obsess about food and eating. Only fat people overeat. Only fat people obsess about their bodies. This fallacy is linked with the idea that being slim means that one is also mentally healthy.

> *This reminds me of a woman I used to work with named Marion. She was perfectly slender. No worries about what kinds of foods she ate or what amounts. But how did she feed herself? Mostly with junk foods, high fat and sugar foods. She rarely ate what would be described as wholesome, natural foods. She didn't like cooking, so she hardly ever prepared meals. Marion just grabbed whatever was convenient. She also had several food cravings which she would indulge (chocolate being one of them). She could sit at her desk and polish off four chocolate bars in one tea break. If there was any food item that she fancied, she was unable to sit still until she procured it. She could be quite neurotic about it. And to top it off, she was constantly declaring her dissatisfaction with her figure. Needless to say, those of us who struggled with our weight wanted to lynch her and tape her mouth shut!*

With the continual increase in eating disorders, I think it can be taken as proved that a person's size is not necessarily indicative of mental well-being. Many bulimics go unnoticed for years because their weight doesn't fluctuate much even though they are abusing their bodies in a very obsessive/compulsive manner. It's just as possible to be large and happy or unhappy as to be small and happy or unhappy. The same goes with being obsessed about weight or food. Children as young as nine and ten are embarking on diets because they view themselves as the wrong shape or size.

FAT FALLACY NO. 6

When I'm thin, my life will be problem-free. The only real problem I have in my life is my weight.

During my early thirties, I had become thinner than even I thought was possible. I remember getting on the scales and being only seven and a half stone. I thought I had arrived in heaven. I had become one of the 'beautiful people'. Four years of hard work and rigid control. Four years of starving and denial, but it was my dream come true. For a fleeting moment anyway. The problem with anorexia is that you keep adjusting your expectations. No matter how much you lose, it is never enough because the body-image distortion keeps telling you that any amount of flesh equals fat. And because I had been so many different weights (and none for very long), I felt my body looked the same within about a two-stone range. I wasn't able to know objectively what I actually looked like. People would say to me, 'You are going to stop losing weight now, aren't you?' and I would say, 'Oh, yes,' but inside I was thinking, 'Are you kidding? I have no intention of stopping, I have never been this thin in my life and I am going to enjoy every moment of it.' The thing was, I wasn't enjoying it.

I derived very little pleasure in my quest for thinness. The fear of gaining weight increased with every pound that I lost. Rituals with food were taken to the extreme. I weighed and measured my food daily, even though I ate exactly the same foods every day! I could have sliced off two ounces of cheese blindfolded. I could have told you the calorie content of a piece of paper. I couldn't look at food on a plate without feeling terror. I wouldn't eat in restaurants because I couldn't weigh and measure my food there. I was hungry most of the time. I filled myself up with coffee and cigarettes. And if I ate more that I had intended, I would torture myself mentally for days. I was very good at self-flagellation. I was driven, and nothing but perfection was acceptable. I rarely enjoyed being with other people because my mind was on what I had eaten or what I was going to eat. There wasn't any room for anyone else in my life. I was truly a woman obsessed. I was constantly preoccupied with food or weight. I might have looked like I was involved in meaningful dialogue with others, but my attention was never free from my body. I lived most of my teenage and adult life feeling that my weight was my problem, and if I could rid myself of it, then I wouldn't have any problems!

I have to say that this is the belief of a great number of intelligent people. We have been so brainwashed by standards and hype that it seems to make sense. This emotional blackmail can cloud even a highly functioning person's perspectives.

Why do people eat?

Let's consider why people eat. Do you think that people eat simply out of hunger? I'm sure you've noticed that you don't always eat because you're hungry. We eat for myriad reasons. People often think that it is only the overweight who eat for reasons other than hunger. This is simply not true! You're not alone, so don't believe for even one minute that there is something unique about how you use food. Think of all the holiday eating that occurs simply because it's Christmas!

In different places, at different times, people use food for something other than pure nourishment. Everyone likes to enjoy food. There is nothing wrong with liking the taste of food! And once more, as the research in *Eating Habits* by Boakes, Popplewell and Burton concludes, much of our learning and behaviour around food is acquired in childhood. The types of food we choose, how much we eat and the associations that we make with food are not born out of the mind of a compulsive eater but are learned responses; some innate, some from social interactions and some from the experience of eating itself.

Esther grew up in a household where eating everything on your plate was the expected behaviour at meals. Even if she was full up, she still had to finish what was left. And if she didn't eat everything put in front of her, then she didn't get any pudding. To this day, even when she is the one loading her plate, she feels obliged to eat everything on it.

Gillian grew up during the Second World War when food rationing was in force, so sugary items and puddings were rare and special treats. She has often felt that her attraction to sweet foods is connected with the feeling of being able to have what she wants on demand.

Rebecca's cultural and religious upbringing was Jewish. In her family, the preparing and eating of food played a significant part in her socialisation. Meals could go on for hours at a time. There was always much more available than one could eat. Food wasn't just a meal, it was an event! And the eating of it all was a celebration. It was a grand time with friends and relatives. Food has many happy associations for Rebecca.

Food is used for many different reasons: for comfort, for energy, for pleasure, as a source of nurturing, as a special treat, as a form of socialising.

On a cold day, something warm can be quite comforting, just as on a hot day, something cool can be really refreshing. A lot of people feel safe and comfortable when they have a full stomach. Everyone attaches certain qualities of comfort to certain foods and what they feel they do for them. Everyone eats to some degree for the sheer sensation of tasting good food. We don't eat just because we know it's good for us! We eat things that taste good because it's pleasurable.

Some people eat when they are feeling shaky or a bit out of sorts. Food can make them feel more like they have their feet planted firmly on the ground. It can make them feel less mentally or emotionally confused. It is one reason why students are advised to eat something in the protein or carbohydrate range before taking an exam. They need to have some food to fuel their brains. Eating certain foods at particular times can have a very positive affect on the body.

Because eating in general is a pleasurable activity, people use it as a way to treat themselves when they want to feel special or relieved or rewarded. We like to give ourselves pleasure, and there is nothing wrong with deriving pleasure from eating!

> *At one of my birthday parties, my friends made me an ice-cream cake because they knew it was my favourite dessert. When they presented it to me, they also gave me a very small teaspoon to eat it with because they knew I would want to savour every single bite!*

The problem isn't really that we use food for these different reasons. The problem is that those who are compulsive in their behaviour tend to go over the top in their sensitivity to eating. We have a very black or white mentality for everything. 'Well, if I've started to eat the biscuits, I might as well eat until the tin is empty because I've already blown it!' or 'I'll eat everything I want to today because tomorrow I'm going to start my new diet and I'll never eat this bad stuff again!' Not particularly realistic thinking is it? Remember that it is your deprivation anxiety (diet mentality) that sets up this type of response. The mind is very clever. It is easy to live with delusions so that we can rationalise our behaviour and desires.

> *When I was first married, I used cooking for my husband as an excuse for me to eat. I thought, 'Right, I'm married now, wives are supposed to cook nice things for their husbands.' Of course, the things that I chose to prepare were the things that I really wanted to eat. I didn't ask him what he wanted! I began making treats under the guise of nurturing, when in fact I wanted a reason to concoct some goodies for myself.*

Do you recognise when you use food to do something other than take away your hunger? We often attach personal attributes to food that are completely unrealistic. Can food really make you feel better emotionally in the long term? Is it really a substitute for mum, or love or not being lonely? What does food mean to you? Take a look at the adverts and see how they represent food. What do they tell us about food? There is one advert I remember that has to do with a brand of instant coffee.

The scene is a woman driving up to a cliff overlooking the ocean. Dawn is about to break. She is visibly upset by something and a tear is rolling down her face. She reaches into the back seat of her car and finds a jar of coffee. She pulls out a mug, some bottled water and a heating element that she can plug into her cigarette lighter. She brews herself a cup of coffee right there in her car. She then gets out of her car and, as the sun is rising, she is sipping her coffee with a look of relief and satisfaction on her face. The lyrics of the song in the background are, 'I can see clearly now the rain has gone . . . all obstacles slip away . . . it's gonna be a bright, bright, sunshiny day.' As if one cup of coffee could turn her entire emotional state around or change the direction of her day!

Coffee is a stimulant and an addictive substance (we will talk about addictive foods later on). It can pep her up for a while. But, as with all food used to alter a mood, it is just a temporary solution.

Food is greatly overrated in terms of what it can do for you. All food can do is nourish the body and take away hunger. It is not some coercive substance that can chain you to a chair and force itself down your throat. We do tend to treat it as if it has some magical or evil properties. It is only food! You need to get out of the frame of mind that allows you to think that food is controlling you. It is just an inert object. Most of the food people eat is not even living food. It's just dead roughage. So stop thinking that it's something that can control you. You are in charge of what you do. Food can't call to you from the cupboard and make you come and eat it! It's your own overblown idea and your own anxiety that make you feel you are not in control of what you do with food.

When do people eat?

There are lots of situations that make people feel like turning to food. Do you know what feelings or circumstances make you feel like eating? Do you ever stop to take stock of what you're feeling *before* you turn to food? Is eating an unconscious and automatic reaction to your mood or emotional state? Do you eat to live or live to eat?

People often eat for many emotional reasons. Most of the time they don't even know why they are eating because their response is so mechanical and quick. Do any of the reasons below sound familiar to you?

People turn to food . . .

- when they are anxious;
- when they feel stressed;
- when they are depressed and want a little pick-me-up;
- to fill an emotional void;
- to fill time;
- to reward themselves;
- as an unconscious habit — just a hand-to-mouth instant reaction (they do this without thinking at all — it's just mechanical);
- as compulsive behaviour triggered by an addictive substance, such as sugar, coffee or chocolate;
- out of **mouth hunger**. They see or smell something that looks as though it would taste good and they simply want to eat it for the taste sensation that it will produce. They may not even be hungry, but they are stimulated by their other senses.

How often do you eat out of real hunger, when your stomach is empty and you are in need of more energy? Do you even experience true hunger, or is it all mouth hunger? If you eat repeatedly when you are not hungry or when you are already full, you really confuse your body. It doesn't know what kind of messages to give to the brain, because you are constantly overriding what is actually occurring. Many of us are not even sure if we have appetites! A lot of people assume that anorexics don't have big appetites, but in fact the opposite is true. They get so hungry, they think they will lose control if they eat anything. They constantly override their body's natural cues.

In *Fighting Food – Coping with Eating Disorders*, Lawrence and Dana describe a compulsive eater as someone who overeats for reasons other than physical hunger. Emotional states and external cues become confused with the body's natural sensations. The compulsive eater interprets most discomfort, whether physical or emotional, as a cue for eating. No matter what the situation, the compulsive eater automatically turns to food as the solution.

Food anaesthetises feelings

Many of my clients report that they are so disconnected from their bodies that they wonder if they even recognise the signals that their bodies are giving them. And most of them report that, when they overeat or binge, they really taste only the very first bite. The rest just gets shoved down with little or no awareness. I used to have binges that sound exactly like that. I would sit down with a jar of peanut butter and jam, scooping a bit from each jar. Not even knowing why I started to eat, I just started. I would alternate between the two jars for about twenty or thirty minutes. It was very mechanical. There was nothing pleasurable about it. I was simply putting food in my mouth.

Do you decide when to eat, or do you just find yourself eating? Are you aware of what precipitates your overeating? Are you conscious of your reasons for feeling that eating is what you need to do? We have to learn to be aware of what we are doing!

The emotional failure cycle

The frustrating cycle of overeating is something that you are probably very familiar with but have never been able to break. Part of the reason may be because you haven't examined exactly how the cycle gets started. Once it's in place, it's nearly impossible to stop. But you *can* stop it. You need to learn to stop the momentum responsible for its taking off.

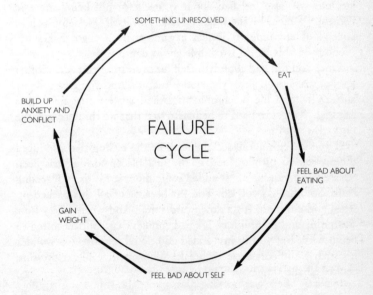

Let's take a look at what comprises this cycle of overeating. The cycle begins to build momentum because there is something that you are not attending to, something that is unresolved or unfelt. And you don't want to acknowledge it or feel it. It doesn't have to be some overpowering emotion or incident; it can be a build-up of little stresses or an uncomfortable feeling in the body. The point is that you don't give yourself any time to respond to your emotional state. Instead, you just react in a mechanical way to try and stop the discomfort and you turn to food to try and relieve yourself of whatever it is you are trying to push down or release. The only problem is that food can only be a momentary distraction from what is really going on, and it can't possibly resolve your feelings or condition.

The next stage of the cycle is you either overeat something that you don't want to or you eat something from your 'bad' list which makes you feel like a failure. Not only do you now feel bad that you ate, but you also feel bad about yourself for not being more in control. (Which, by the way, is a fallacy in itself. None of us is in control of anything. It is just a game that the ego makes up. Nobody in this world is completely in control!)

Once you feel bad about yourself for overeating you add another level of stress to an already anxious situation. And you are probably already living a life of chronic stress and anxiety that never gets released. We get so used to being stressed that we think of it as the normal way to feel.

If you haven't addressed the issue or the feeling that produced the anxiety to turn to food in the first place, nothing has been released and you have just added some more stress to your feeling bank. So what do you do? You eat because of all this backed-up stress and emotion! It's a downward spiral. And we all know how frustrating and painful it is. It's bad enough that you feel rotten to begin with, but you've just added additional tension. No wonder it's such a difficult cycle to break. Who can live like a pressure cooker all the time?

BREAK THE CYCLE

The only way to break out of this cycle is to handle your emotional state from the start. You need to allow yourself to feel what is really going on and give yourself the space to make a decision about what to do with it. We never give ourselves any time, we just tend to react. Stay awake, stay with the discomfort, allow whatever needs to surface to do so. Then you can deal with it and not have to eat over it. We need to take responsibility for our emotions and learn from them. What are they trying to tell you?

One of the reasons that we don't want to deal with our emotions is because we think they'll be overwhelming. We think we'll go out of control with them. But this isn't true. At first it may seem a bit intense when you allow yourself to respond to all the feelings that you have pushed away with food, but it's only because you've stored them instead of releasing them. You must feel the feelings and allow them to be just what they are. Feelings are not in themselves good or bad – they're just feelings. And you don't have to *become* your feelings. You're just afraid of being uncomfortable. But you are going to have to allow yourself to go through some discomfort to come out the other side. Once you get used to letting your feelings surface, you will see that they're not that overpowering and that they will pass. We must be more realistic about what life is like and stop living in this dream world of 'When I'm thin, I'll be perfect' or 'All my problems will disappear'. It just doesn't work like that.

THE SUCCESS CYCLE

None of us is going to reach a point when we won't have to be responsible for ourselves and what we do. You aren't going to get thin and then just stop thinking about what you put in your mouth. You have to be fully awake and conscious all the time. That's the bad news. The good news is that you don't have to keep getting stuck in this cycle of overeating. Just as the failure cycle is self-perpetuating, so is the success cycle.

Either cycle has a run-on effect. The more I allowed myself to be relaxed about who I was and what I looked like, the happier I got. I began to drop the immense struggle I was always having with myself. The happier I got, the more I took better care of myself. The better care I took of myself, the better I felt physically and emotionally. And, of course, the better I began to feel, the more I explored other ways of expanding my relationships and opportunities. The more relaxed I was with myself and food, the more the compulsions ceased!

Next time that you start to go for food, give yourself a moment to think about what you are feeling. Give yourself the time to make a conscious choice. Is food really what you want? Or are you angry or unhappy about something? Food cannot fix anything but hunger! Give yourself a fighting chance! Feel your feelings. It's the only way to stop the cycle before it gets going. Allow your success cycle to become your natural response.

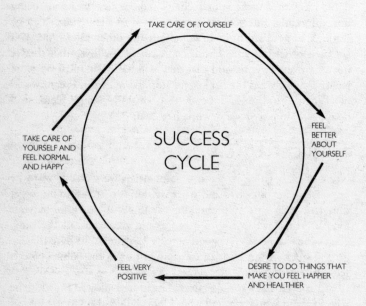

TAKE CARE OF YOURSELF

FEEL BETTER ABOUT YOURSELF

SUCCESS CYCLE

TAKE CARE OF YOURSELF AND FEEL NORMAL AND HAPPY

DESIRE TO DO THINGS THAT MAKE YOU FEEL HAPPIER AND HEALTHIER

FEEL VERY POSITIVE

HOMEWORK

PRACTICAL STEPS

- Continue to observe yourself. Notice how you feel at different times of the day, and with different people.

- Keep a diary of emotions for at least a week. Notice any emotional patterns that you have. Do you have a particular emotional state that seems to pervade your entire day? Write down how you are feeling before you eat. See if there are any recurring patterns to your eating. Observe how you feel before you eat, when you are eating and after you have finished. You don't have to write a lot. Just a sentence or two.

- Continue to notice your breathing in conjunction with how you feel and also while you are eating. Practise taking deep breaths down into your abdomen. Take full breaths while you are eating. Put your fork down in between bites and see how you feel. Relax as much as you can while you are eating.

- Continue to practise guilt-free eating.

WRITTEN EXERCISES

1 Are you able to pin-point specific emotions that seem to precipitate overeating? What gets you started?

2 What did you learn about expressing yourself and showing emotion? Was it all right to show affection or need? Were your parents demonstrative with affection or emotion?

3 How were feelings expressed in your family? How was anger dealt with?

4 Do you express your feelings easily? What don't you want to feel? How do you express fear, sorrow and anger?

5 What have you noticed about your emotions in

relation to your eating behaviour? What is your emotional state before you eat? After you eat?

6 What do you believe about overweight people? Do you see yourself as one of them?

7

'PIGGY-BACKING PROBLEMS' – EXAGGERATING THE DILEMMA

'Piggy-backing problems' is a phrase I use to describe how we create a chain reaction to a single event or state. You are actually adding another problem on top of the one that was originally there. It may seem that the resulting problem is the most prominent because the primary difficulty wasn't resolved. Piggy-backing can happen on an emotional level and on a physical level. (Remember, the body and mind are not separate, no matter how much we relate to them as if they are. If you affect one, then you will almost certainly affect the other in some way.)

There are so many times in life when we have a physical reaction to something emotional or an emotional reaction to something physical. The response may be pleasant or it may be negative. We produce all kinds of these run-on effects without even realising they're connected. And they're not only associated with our weight and eating, but with everything that we do. This cycle can be found in all parts of the body. For example, headaches can be the result of the body's response to emotional tension. However, instead of learning to eliminate or reduce the stress or physical tension that causes the headache, we usually just focus on getting rid of it. It would be far more helpful in the long run to discover ways to prevent them altogether.

Some of our habitual piggy-backing can initiate even more difficulty and pain than the original discomfort.

One of the difficulties that I have with my body is the way that I trained it to respond to anxiety. As you know by now, I always used to feel self-conscious about my body. Because of that, I was very aware of how my body looked at any given time. When I was in school, I would often sit holding my stomach in so that it didn't look fat. I didn't like to breathe into my abdomen because it made it distend. While this is the natural course of things, I didn't like it. I associated anything with making my body bigger as bad or to be avoided. I did this over and over again until breathing normally didn't come naturally to me any more! This started out as an emotional response (feeling self-conscious and anxious about my body) that I translated physically to my body as contraction and withholding my breath. What eventually happened was that whenever I got anxious, I held my breath and bloated up with air. Sometimes it would last for a few weeks because I just couldn't relax enough to release the air. Once I bloated up, I then got anxious because I was sticking out and my body was uncomfortable, so I withheld my breath even more! I could change my size around the waist and abdomen by about an inch and a half (enough to make my clothes tight and uncomfortable) and all through not breathing properly. After years of conditioning myself to that type of response, I am still in the process of retraining myself to breathe into my abdomen and to release my breath.

Let's take a look at how overeating creates a set of piggy-backing problems.

If you do not address the original conflict or emotional state that underlies your discomfort (whether physical or emotional), you may never uncover what it is that actually precipitates your eating behaviour. Say, for instance, that you're frustrated about something and you just can't seem to resolve it. In your impatient state, you turn to food to try to appease yourself. But the food doesn't do

MY WEIGHT MUST
BE A PROBLEM

GAIN WEIGHT
(ADDITIONAL PROBLEM)

FEEL BAD ABOUT SELF
(ADDITIONAL PROBLEM)

EAT
(NON-SUCCESSFUL SOLUTION)

SOMETHING UNRESOLVED

anything other than perhaps taste good for a few bites. Because you are still looking for some type of release, you continue to eat. After you finish, you realise that you still are not satisfied and, in fact, now you are feeling too full and are disgusted with yourself for eating so much. Instead of recognising that you were frustrated to begin with, (but that you haven't sorted that out yet) you may think that you are only eating out of lack of self-control or will-power. Your overeating can then seem complicated and confusing, when in fact you were just frustrated and you didn't know what to do with yourself and all the pent-up energy.

If you eat out of an emotional state and then feel badly that you ate, and especially if you gained weight because of what you ate, you are just accumulating problems. It is easy to think that your weight is the problem because it's at the end of a string of complications. But it's not really the problem – it only looks that way because it was the last thing in line! Your weight isn't your problem. Your problem is how you cope in general.

In *Eating Disorders*, Bruch demonstrates how overeating and gaining weight generate some secondary psychological problems that weren't there to begin with. For example, you think that being overweight isn't acceptable. Therefore, if you are, it makes you feel inferior, which in turn makes you a bit paranoid that everyone is watching your figure or your eating habits. Compulsive eating chips away at a person's self-esteem and confidence. Even if you didn't feel inferior before you started dieting, believe me you will once you've finished, because you're going to fail. You're going to put the weight back on, which makes you unacceptable again. You start to take on a new and negative identity for yourself.

Self-esteem

Reading literature by well-educated clinicians and behaviouralists, I am appalled by their continued advice to people to go on diets or to slimming groups. Aside from the fact that they don't work, there is something so sterile, so unfeeling and so derogatory about this advice. How can anyone maintain any kind of self-worth when the majority of society wants to get rid of them?

Self-esteem is a very large component in the compulsive eating syndrome. There is some reason why you already feel inadequate in the world. This is one reason that looking at your **Oedipal history** is so important. Your beliefs were established in your very early days. This is not an attempt to blame your parents – this is just a fact. Most of the formative influences in your life happened before you could talk. That's why it is so difficult to change the way we see ourselves. But you must put a great deal of energy into changing how you see yourself. And I don't mean just by trying to convince yourself that you are all right, whether you actually believe it or not. You need to start believing that you are fine exactly as you are. You need to effect a change between your mind, your emotions and your body.

First of all, you must take a look at why it is that you think you are so inadequate. What did you do that was so terrible? You treat yourself as if you were a criminal or someone needing to be punished. **Compulsive eating is not a crime!** It's just a type of behaviour that you adopted at some point and it simply doesn't serve you. You must stop treating yourself so harshly and develop some compassion for yourself. Do you allow yourself to be human? Stop thinking it's OK for others to make mistakes or have shortcomings, but not you! What are your expectations for yourself? Are they realistic? Why are you working so hard to prove that you are not worth loving? You'll never be able to get it right. There's no right way to be or act. You can't please everyone all the time – you'd be fighting a losing battle even to try. It would be much more beneficial if you spent your time taking good care of yourself and letting who you are be felt and heard. You haven't done anything wrong – you are simply struggling with your weight, and you have blown the struggle all out of proportion, Your conflict doesn't need to be with food. It's with yourself. You must remember that you're not crazy or inadequate, you're just compulsive!

Helen is a young woman of nineteen. She has been overweight her entire life. Although she has worked very hard to maintain a sense of self-esteem throughout years of ridicule, life is a constant struggle between developing a positive identity and her extreme self-consciousness. Fearful of negative attention from others, she often belittles herself in public. Her logic is that if she refers to her weight first, then others won't bring up the subject. If she acknowledges that she has a weight problem, then she hopes others will leave her alone. Helen hopes this will save her some emotional pain. It doesn't. In fact, it makes her feel worse about herself because she is continually berating herself publicly or privately. She has also got herself into a real dilemma about eating in public. She feels she can't be seen to be eating 'diet food' (anything nutritious, salads, etc.) or people will assume she's dieting. This would be an admission of her guilt as a fat person. But she also doesn't think she can be seen to eat 'junk foods' or 'forbidden for fatties foods' either or people will think, 'Why, isn't that just like a fat person, no wonder she's big, look at what's she's eating!'

You must begin to stand up for yourself. It's not appropriate for people to make comments about your weight or what you are eating. And you're the one that's going to have to tell them so! It's not all right for people to ridicule you about your weight or your eating. It's insensitive, it's rude and it's none of their business! And if it wasn't for the fact that you believed you really had done something wrong, you wouldn't let them get away with it!

You were duped. You were duped into believing that dieting was going to give you long-term weight loss. But it can't. And you have been brainwashed into thinking that if dieting didn't work for you, then it's because you somehow fell short. Instead of worrying about what others think about your weight, you need to pay attention to how you can get what you need and desire.

Common characteristics

There are some common personality traits that people who are compulsive eaters tend to share. (These also fit other eating disorders as well as frustrated dieters.) I realise that these are generalisations, but I have seen them so frequently over the years that they're worth looking at.

LOW SELF-ESTEEM

This one is very common with women. We place far too much emphasis on the superficial aspects of ourselves and our lives. We put a lot of energy into how we look and what we can cook. We put everyone else first, and if we think of doing nice things for ourselves, we feel we're being selfish or greedy. We're not taught self-esteem. We're taught to compete and to compare ourselves with others. This produces a losing battle, because there will always be someone cleverer, richer or prettier. And if your worth is tied up with how you look, you are continually going to be disappointed, because everyone ages. There is no way to stop the ageing process, so you will become less and less satisfied with yourself as time goes on.

BLACK-AND-WHITE THINKING

Because we tend to be somewhat exaggerated characters (blowing things out of proportion), our behaviour can get exaggerated as well. We tend to feel things must be either all one way or another. Things are either really good or really bad. We don't seem to operate within a middle ground very often. One reason is because it's not as exciting to be ordinary. And it's also easier to be fanatical and rigid about something than it is to be moderate. Moderation can seem like nothing is happening.

LOW FRUSTRATION TOLERANCE

This means that we are basically impatient people. We want

everything immediately. And if things don't go smoothly or as expected, we get frustrated and want to give up. This, coupled with 'black-and-white thinking', has stopped many a person from realising their full potential.

CHILDISH ORIENTATION TO LIFE

Many of us depend on our external circumstances to give us happiness. We think that something outside ourselves determines whether or not we are having a good day or a bad day, or whether or not we are acceptable or lovable. We blame others for things that don't go right. We use a lot of 'if onlys'. We're not being fully responsible for ourselves and our actions. We want magic, miracle cures.

OVERLY SENSITIVE

Being sensitive is a wonderful quality. But compulsive people can have a tendency to go over the top with it. Because we don't have a good sense of ourselves, we look to others for validation. We're self-conscious and take things very personally. A single glance or phrase by someone can send us reeling into self-doubt. We feel everyone is watching us and think that somehow everything revolves around our weight. This is a concept that gets blown completely out of proportion. However, no one in the general public really cares what you weigh. I mean it. They don't. At the end of the day, no one but you cares about your weight. People simply don't have the time to have their attention on you all day. They're too busy with their own lives. We have to leave this paranoid thinking behind. You're wasting a lot of time and energy trying to please all the wrong people.

IMPULSIVE/COMPULSIVE

I bet I don't have to explain this one! We've all experienced feeling that uncontrollable urge to do something quickly. Almost as if it's the immediacy that's important. This covers everything from making impulsive purchases to eating without thinking. What sets this apart from just plain impatience is the mysterious and potent driving force that generates its momentum.

Before you start thinking that you must be a terrible person if those are the descriptive qualities of your personality, please note that this is only a partial list! All people have their rough edges and their more endearing qualities. Qualities aren't in themselves good or bad. They just are what they are. It's when they get out of balance one way or another that they cause difficulty. You must allow yourself to be realistic. We're all just human beings. We all have the same range of feelings and hopes and desires. We must begin to love ourselves as the fragile and wonderful beings that we are.

LEARN TO LOVE YOURSELF

I have many clients who are always trying to please others. Their days are filled with projects and favours they are doing for their friends and families. They feel compelled to do, do, do. They put themselves last (at best) or not at all. Some of this has to do with feeling that they won't be liked or valued or accepted if they don't placate others. Some of it has to do with completely ignoring their own wants and needs because they don't think of their needs as worthwhile.

> *Delia is on the go from morning until night. She is busy trying to make sure that her three children and her neighbours and friends are happy, entertained and not put out in any way. She feels driven to keep everyone content. Obviously she has very little time left over for herself. She has often said that she doesn't know how to say no to people. And sometimes it escalates to the point that she resents all the things she is doing for others but still feels unable to release any of it. This keeps her feeling inadequate because she can't make everyone happy, and since she doesn't spend any time on herself she never feels good about herself. She has compassion for everyone except herself.*

Develop compassion and understanding for yourself. Begin to love yourself. That is not a selfish or conceited thing. No one is better than anyone else. We are all in the same boat. We all want to be loved and feel included. There's no way of winning. Stop playing life as if you can win! Nowhere, at any time, will there be someone crowned as the richest, thinnest, best human being. It just isn't going to happen. Yet you stake your whole worth on what you look like. Is your weight the most important thing to you in life? What about people, relationships, loving? Don't you have better things to do than constantly worry about your body? We have the determination of will to achieve great things if put to positive use. But when we focus solely on the body we tend to implode. I was certainly willing to forgo my health in the pursuit of thinness. I did everything to be thin. Begin to focus your attention on what's in front of you. Put energy into what you want to get out of life, not on a few qualities that throw you out of balance.

Addictive behaviour

In the *Handbook of Psychotherapy for Anorexia and Bulimia*, Garner and Garfinkel's research has concluded that the 'dieting-bingeing-purging cycle is self-perpetuating . . .' In other words, it becomes an addictive behaviour. Whether you happen to purge after overeating or not, I believe that the cycle for overeating can also be an addictive behaviour. It has that inexplicable impulsive/compulsive drive behind it. The aimless searching for fulfilment or satisfaction. Very often people find themselves overeating when it is the last thing that they want to do. 'Much of an addict's mental obsession results from denial or refusing to recognise the loss of control that is happening on the emotional level' (*The Addictive Personality* by Craig Nakken). All addiction has this out-of-control quality. And with all addictions, the behaviour becomes progressive. Addictions don't get better with time, they get worse. And no matter how much you are able to indulge in your addiction, it is never enough.

When I was pursuing thinness at all costs, I decided to take my own meals with me wherever I went. I thought it would take the worry out of eating. I was completely rigid about my new plan because I knew that I could not trust myself to be spontaneous with food. I weighed and measured my food daily. I did not deviate from my eating plan in four years (except for a very rare binge). I prepared the same food each day. I wasn't just religious in my fervour to be thin, I was becoming addicted to the process of weighing and measuring my food. I was terrified to eat in restaurants because I had no control over the portions served, so I hardly ever ate out. A few of my friends said they admired my tenacity; it may have started out as determination, but it turned into bondage. I was filled with trepidation. I felt compelled to weigh everything. On the outside, it seemed that I was more in control than I had ever been, but on the inside I was an addict waiting to go over the top at any moment.

When I was in my mid-twenties, I heard about a group called Overeaters Anonymous. They are a self-help group that meets all around the world. They follow the same format as Alcoholics Anonymous. Their programme works on the premise that you're addicted to your eating behaviour and that you're not in control of that behaviour. Instead of trying to use will-power to diet, you're supposed to 'surrender to a power greater than yourself'. In effect, you have to ask for divine intervention. This intervention doesn't have to come from God, but from whatever or whoever you consider a force greater than yourself in the universe. I found their meetings to be very helpful and attended them for a number of years because I felt that I definitely had an addictive-type personality. Part of what I learned from the meetings was that I was not alone in my compulsive behaviour and that there were many other people who understood my suffering. The group also helped me to express my feelings so I wouldn't end up eating because of them. Information on this group is given in the Helpful People section.

Have you ever thought of your eating behaviour as obsessive? Have a look at your eating cycles. Do they have any of this repetitive element in them? Do you have a mental obsession with bingeing or eating certain foods? There are also such things as addictive foods, and they can make an enormous difference to your eating behaviour. We'll look at this in more detail in chapter 9.

HOMEWORK

PRACTICAL STEPS

- Continue to observe your behaviour in relation to your feelings. Remember that you're not doing this because you're stupid or because you're doing something wrong. You're collecting information about yourself so that you can alter what doesn't work for you any more.

- Continue to practise deeper breathing and to notice your breath in relation to eating.

- Begin to stand up for yourself if people are rude to you. You don't have to be aggressive or rude back. You can simply inform them that their comment hurt and was out of line. Take an **assertiveness** class!

- Begin to do things that will help increase your self-esteem. Pamper yourself. You don't have to spend a lot of time or money to do this. Grab a friend and swap facials, paint your toenails. Get a make-over. Take bubble baths, look for places that you can buy clothes that fit properly. Begin reading material that is supportive (you may find some things in the Resources section).

- Write letters to the shops that don't stack your size. Write to anyone or any company that needs to have their consciousness raised.

WRITTEN EXERCISES

1 Do you eat in secret? Do you feel you can't be seen eating what you really want?

2 Do you feel that your behaviour around food is out of control? Are you aware of your eating patterns or do you just find yourself overeating?

3 Are you able to distinguish between 'mouth hunger' and stomach hunger?

4 Do you avoid social occasions due to food?

5 Make a list of your qualities and characteristics. Under each one, write how it can be both a benefit and a hindrance to you.

105

8

NOW THAT I HAVE THESE HABITS, HOW DO I CHANGE THEM?

>   *'All of the ways by which people stimulate themselves – including everything from jogging to cigarettes and sex – are expressions of the same fundamental error: people do not live already in the Fullness of Life. They live in problems, anxieties, contractions, emptiness; they have dull minds, and they act only via the stimulation of mechanical tendencies.'*

[From a talk entitled 'The Fullness of Life' included in *The Eating Gorilla Comes in Peace* by Adi Da copyright (Avatara Dau Loloma Pty. Ltd., as trustee for the Avatara Dau Loloma Sacred Trust). Used with permission.]

Overeating, or compulsive eating, doesn't occur by chance, though it can occur quite unconsciously. If you continue to repeat a certain behaviour each time a stimulus is introduced, you will soon create a repetitive pattern, whether you were paying attention or not! And, if we allow ourselves to respond without thinking, we may develop habits that we don't want. Part of the reason is because the body has a physical memory as well as an emotional memory. The physical memory is one of the reasons why people can learn to do athletics and physical activity without having to be retrained every time they want to repeat that activity. How else do you think that dancers can learn routines? It's not just their mind identifying with the steps, but also their muscles remembering the action. But your emotional memory serves to create the driving force behind your reactions.

We respond this way in everything we do, from very simple tasks to very emotionally loaded situations and a host of circumstances in between. For instance, it can be as easy as turning off a light switch. Let's say you've decided that you want to save energy and money by turning the lights off each time you leave a room. At first, you'll have to concentrate to remind yourself that this is a new habit that you want to develop. The first few times you leave a room, you'll have to prompt yourself. But at some point, if turning off the lights is sufficiently important to you, then you'll begin to do it automatically. Before you know it, you'll be routinely hitting the light switch without thinking before walking out the door.

A more emotionally charged example of this same idea can be seen in animals (or people, for that matter) when they have been abused. If an animal is mistreated, it will have an emotional and physical response to the cues that mean it's about to be harmed again. Say it's been hit a lot. Every time the animal sees a hand coming towards it, it will feel fear. It will either cower (become frozen in its fear) or it will fight back. Emotionally and physically, it's expecting to be hurt again. And it responds according to the state that it's in at any given moment. Each time it feels it's in the same circumstances, it will repeat this behaviour. Animals and people are creatures of habit. The body and the mind remember and respond.

This is how the pattern works: first there is something that arouses you. You may or may not be consciously aware of this stimulation. But your body is going to respond to it regardless. Then your body and emotions attach memory to this stimulus and act according to your previous experience with it. The consequence of your reaction may or may not be what you hoped to achieve, but you can be sure that it has acted as a reinforcer for the future. This reinforcement may be either negative or positive. There doesn't need to be a positive outcome in order to repeat something. And in fact, negative reinforcement often seems more powerful than positive. But if you decide that you don't like the consequence of your response, then you must create a new memory in association with that stimulus so you can create a different response.

> STIMULUS > MEMORY (physical, emotional) > RESPONSE

The good news is that you are completely trainable, no matter what your age! Behaviours are learned and they can be relearned. Habits are only mechanical reactions that we play out over and over again. They are difficult to break because we have practised them so many times that they become automatic. And because emotionally you *feel* they are set in concrete, you don't think that they can be altered.

Reinvent yourself

In order to produce different behaviour, you have to begin to see yourself differently. You can't continue to identify yourself in a negative way. Nor can you meditate on the negative image that you associate with yourself because of your actions. You are not bad or stupid or wrong because of what you do or don't eat. This is an absurd notion and yet many live by this principle. You must begin to create a new identity for yourself. The silly part of this is that you don't really have to make up a new you. You simply have to let the happy one inside free. She's been held hostage far too long! Concentrating on 'Oh, I'm fat, I'm fat, I'm fat' isn't going to get anyone thin. If you want to be a 'normal-size' person, then you can't meditate on being overweight. The more you focus your attention on the negative, the more you reinforce it. If you constantly think of yourself as fat, you will become it. If you believe that your habits and tendencies are irrevocable, then you will never be able to change them.

I've had numerous experiences with this concept. The more down, depressed and anxious I was about my weight, the more of a problem it became. I seemed to gain weight for no reason. This made me even more unhappy with myself, which in turn made me hate myself more and take even less care of myself. It was a downward spiral. But I also noticed the reverse happen. The more I stopped worrying about my food, the less I compulsively overate, the happier I became, the freer I felt and the less weight I carried around. Call me crazy, but it's true!

Discipline your attention

To change behaviour that you don't like, you must begin to practise forgiveness and focusing your attention. You must also begin to see yourself in a new light. When it comes to your eating behaviour, you probably already have a tendency to feel that the patterns you've established are wrong. This doesn't help you to change them. They're not wrong, they were just the best alternative you could come up with at the time. You must remember that you thought these patterns would help or you wouldn't have adopted them. So don't beat yourself up over them. The point is that your current pattern of behaviour is simply not serving you in a positive way any more, so it is time to modify it. You want to develop patterns of behaviour that help you grow and feel good about yourself. Enough of this self-destructiveness. Most of us only create ways to feel bad about ourselves, not to feel good. Feeling guilty about coming off a diet or overeating never did anyone any bit of good. And no one ever became a better person through of this type of thinking.

You also need to give yourself some time. You developed these patterns and ways of coping over a period of time and have been reinforcing them ever since. Struggling with yourself only reinforces your self-possession. You won't be able to make huge and complete changes overnight. You must be patient with yourself; you have taken a long time to establish your patterns and train the people around you, so you need time to relearn and retrain yourself, just as the people around you will need some time to adapt to the new you. Instead, take responsibility for your emotions and actions. Learn from them. What have they been trying to tell or teach you?

BE NICER TO YOUR 'INNER CHILD'

You must also be nicer to your 'little child' within. She did the best she could with what she had. You developed your patterns to survive the environment you grew up in the best way you could. You have to understand that most of your coping habits were designed by the mind of a child. A child who had an emotional response to the relationships and circumstances around her. She didn't have the reasoning capacity of the adult mind to sort out what was subjective and what was objective. So you need to give yourself a break. Your little child came up with the best that she could. It's just that these patterns don't work anymore. They're not getting you what you want, which is to be relaxed about food and let your body get its balance back.

Another thing that you must remember is that you are never going to reach a plateau where you can just stop being conscious and responsible. Everyone wants to get rid of whatever it is that's bothering them, then never have to think about it again. But life isn't like that. There will always be things to handle. There will always be emotional upsets and things that get out of control. You may think that if you don't diet, you'll go out of control. This is another fallacy. The more you relax, the more you will eat moderately and the more you will release this stress from your body.

LOSE CONTROL!

People whose eating is distressed tend to have a lot of worries about control. We feel we must hold the reins tight or everything will fall to pieces. We're not very good with moderation or spontaneity. Again, this goes back to our black-and-white approach to life. Knowing that you're not in control of everything can be quite freeing, if you let it. You don't have to worry about running the whole world any more or taking care of everyone else's feelings! And if you weren't so dissociated from your body, you could relax and know that it isn't trying to work against you. I found it to be quite a relief that I didn't have to worry about every little thing any more because I couldn't make a difference to most things anyway!

And this was crucial in my beginning to lose weight and have my body get its balance back. I surrendered my control; I let it go. It's made my life so much simpler and natural and happy.

    ❖ *'For every action there is an equal and opposite reaction.'* ❖

Albert Einstein

People often say to me, 'All I really want to do is lose weight. That is the most important thing to me.' And I have to say, 'If that were really all you wanted to do, you would have done it already.' You're intelligent people. You would have figured this out long ago if it were so obvious. For people who have put so much energy and attention into losing weight, doesn't it strike you as odd that you're not at the weight you want to be? That in itself should lead you to suspect that weight has more to do with things other than just input versus output.

The quote above from Einstein is one of the explanations why you're not the weight you want to be or why you're a compulsive eater. If you're not where you want to be, then it means that there's something working against you. This is the opposite reaction. You probably don't even know what it is. But you can be sure that it carries precisely as much force as your desire to be thinner. And this is part of the puzzle that you have to unravel for yourself. You must discover what it is that is coming at you from the opposite direction. I'll give you an example of how this law of physics operates in normal daily life.

Frances has queried why her attempts at weight loss have not been successful, even though she has spent most of her adult life in this pursuit. She feels dreadful and unlovable because of her size. Her self-consciousness and reduced self-esteem make going out in public a humiliating experience. She is also in a marriage that has lost its reason for continuing, other than the fact that there are children to consider. When we began to examine her feelings about herself and her life situation, we discovered the energy that was opposing her. She recognised a very large emotional dilemma that was holding her weight in place. On the surface, of course she wanted to lose weight and be free of compulsive eating. She wanted to be light and attractive. But on the other hand, she felt if she lost weight, then she would become promiscuous. Her suppressed sexual feelings frightened her. She felt she would go out of control with them. She felt if she got thin, she would want to go looking for a new mate. Even though she was unhappy in her marriage, she didn't want to face the possibility of it breaking up because she didn't feel she was worthy of anything better. At some point, Frances needs to decide what is more important to her. She needs to allow herself to enter the unknown. She needs to decide where she wants to put her energy. She can't know what will happen. But suppressing herself keeps her stuck.

Once you've changed your act, you need never look back

People don't realize just how trainable they actually are. Every day, in lots of little ways, you are teaching yourself new things. New ways of responding to people and situations. But for some reason, the more modern we become, the less we rely on our own instincts, our own decisions. We are constantly looking for guarantees or confirmation *before* we act. We don't trust ourselves very much at all. But why should you think that you would go completely out of control if you let your body or heart do the directing? This is the natural order of things.

So many of my clients fear that, if they were to trust themselves to make the appropriate decisions about food, they would let themselves down. They don't think that they are trustworthy. They doubt themselves and their own instincts. This is partly because they have become quite dissociated from their bodies. They don't see themselves as a complete entity. They have become so used to overriding their natural responses that they don't think they have any positive internal guidance. They don't think that anyone is on their side, not even themselves! This is preposterous. Their only problem is being separate from their hearts and bodies. Because of this, they often react to situations immediately and only think about what they have done later. With this type of automatic impulse influencing their behaviour, they end up looking back with regret, wishing they could have done things differently. This happens a lot with compulsive eating. We don't quite know what to do with ourselves, so we start putting food into our mouths before we have worked out what we feel or want. One way to break this reaction is to:

> **FEEL** what is going on
> **THINK** about what you want to do about it
> *THEN* **RESPOND**

Feelings affect behaviour

Feelings are very important when we're trying to sort out behaviour that we don't want, because feelings initiate behaviour. Until you begin to recognise your uneasiness and deal with it, you can't hope to change the behaviour that it precipitates.

If we're looking for an outlet for our uncomfortableness, food is an easy and ready alternative. The only problem with using food as a solution to emotional issues is that it ultimately can't make you feel better emotionally or psychologically. It can only cure hunger. So you will always be left with the original discomfort.

At first, it may seem difficult to figure out what you are feeling, especially if you've repressed a lot of your feelings. I know that in my case, if I didn't talk about what was bothering me, the energy would build and eventually I would eat because of it. It takes some practice to decipher feelings and release them. If you're not used to expressing your feelings, it will take a while until you feel comfortable doing this. Chances are that you've been more used to trying *not* to feel your feelings or to express yourself. Expressing yourself is definitely important, but you don't have to tell everyone about how you feel in order to do this. You can also express and release feelings by writing about them, doing something creative with them or doing something physical.

Don't put yourself last

Often women are so used to nurturing everyone around them that they forget to take care of themselves. Or they always attend to themselves last. People often think that it is conceited to think of themselves first, but that couldn't be further from the truth. If you don't take care of yourself, then you have very little to give others. Wouldn't you rather go to others already feeling fulfilled rather than feeling like you just have to hang in there until you can get a quiet moment to yourself? This is a big reason why women eat and overeat. They are trying to feel nurtured or fulfilled or they are trying to keep their stamina up or give themselves a break or a treat.

How to change behaviour

Let's get down to the fundamentals necessary to change a pattern. Just as you taught yourself to use food in situations other than being truly hungry, you must learn alternative ways of dealing with these circumstances. So how do you set about changing things?

In order to change a habit you're going to have to invest about thirty days consciously trying to alter it. It takes the body and mind about this amount of repetition to make the change long lasting. I have devised an acronym that will help you to remember how to go about changing any pattern. I refer to it as coming up for AIR. This stands for Awareness, Investment and Redecision.

AIR = Awareness, Investment, Redecision

AWARENESS

Before you can change anything, you have to be aware of what you're doing. We've talked about this briefly before. Often habits are so unconscious and automatic that you don't even notice that you're doing them, especially with compulsive eating. Overeating often begins out of some unconscious, hand-to-mouth action. You start eating without even realising what you're doing. Then it becomes too late once you're started. You're not sure why you're eating, but you just can't seem to stop. So the very first step in breaking a pattern is to observe what you actually do. This sounds simpler than it is. People don't always want to look at what they actually do because then they feel bad about themselves. The point is not to notice what you do so that you can flagellate yourself with it, but so that you can become conscious and responsible. In this way, you choose what you are going to do.

INVESTMENT

The next step in changing any pattern is to uncover what makes you continue that particular pattern of behaviour. You must be getting something out of the action, or you wouldn't continue it. There is some type of reinforcement going on. Remember, the reinforcement doesn't have to be positive to be effective. For example, compulsive eating generally makes a person feel bad about themselves. They feel they have failed or let themselves down or that they just aren't able to be 'normal' about food. If you see yourself as an inadequate person, then compulsive eating just confirms what you already think of yourself. So overeating becomes a very potent, negative reinforcement for feeling bad about yourself.

115

If you want to prove to yourself that you're weak, then all you have to do is eat compulsively. This is probably not something that you are doing consciously. Generally, we're quite unconscious about our motives. The problem with this type of unconscious operating is that it was developed very early on in life and it doesn't serve you any longer. Instead of feeling that you have wasted time or being hard on yourself for the type of behaviour that you have chosen, you need to be compassionate with yourself. You have developed your tendencies for very good reasons. And you wouldn't have come to these realisations any earlier than when you were ready to explore them. But if you feel that some of your actions are holding you back, then you need to take a look at their binding power. Ask yourself what you are getting out of each of the patterns you want to break. Is it making you happier? What do you really want? Is your action producing the desired results?

It may be that discontinuing a particular behaviour may be too scary for you. Or you simply may not be ready or able to give it up. I had one woman on my course who stopped coming after three weeks. She told me that she couldn't continue the course because she didn't feel she was ready to let go of her eating patterns and she was too afraid to think about changing them. It was right for her to leave because otherwise she would have felt guilty that she wasn't up to it and she would have compared herself to the other women in the class who *were* ready to move on. You must do things at your own pace.

In examining your investment in your behaviour, you may also find that you're getting a lot out of continuing it. It may be that what you are getting out of continuing is a more powerful reinforcement than what you would get if you discontinued it.

Most compulsive eaters express their disgust at their apparent lack of will-power with food. But I know that there's much more than that involved to prompt such erratic and out-of-control behaviour. You must discover what you are getting out of compulsive eating before you can realistically make any difference to it. This brings us to the last component in changing patterns, Redecision.

REDECISION

After you have uncovered your investment in a particular pattern of behaviour or habit, you need to give yourself the space to decide what you want to do about it. You need to feel that you are making a conscious choice to continue it or work on releasing it. Most people usually feel that they should discontinue some behaviour without any understanding about why they do it in the first place. All this does is reinforce negative feelings about themselves and it's a set-up for failure. You must avoid setting yourself up to fail. There is no reason that you should feel bad about what you do. It's just a habit that's had a lot of reinforcement. You can change any habit once you have some understanding about why you chose to do it.

It may be that the investment in continuing the behaviour outweighs the advantages of discontinuing it. This is also where redecision comes in. You have to allow it to be all right to continue something that you're not ready or willing to give up without feeling guilty or bad about it. You'll give it up when you can see that you are the one suffering from it. If you're not ready, just accept the fact. You have to have a reason to give it up. Look at your investments. Juggle the pros and cons of continuing or discontinuing your behaviour. Redecide what you want to do about it and then let whatever you decide be all right. If you decide that you still need to continue a behaviour, but you feel guilty about your decision, you're just setting yourself up to fail again. You need to have the freedom to choose what is right for you at the moment. It doesn't mean that you may not be ready to give it up in the future. Everyone must do what they need to in their own time. The initial steps in changing a pattern are already laid out because you have observed what you do and you recognise what you get out of doing it. You can't make any changes without first going through these two steps. Give yourself the freedom to make your own choices – that in itself opens up some space so that you can change – but your decisions need to be realistic.

Change is scary for everyone

When you're making changes to yourself, it can be quite threatening to those around you simply because they're not sure how to react. They might not feel they know how to respond to you any more. So you need to take them through a retraining programme as well! You trained them to respond to you in a certain way initially and now you need to train them to respond in a way parallel to the way you are growing and changing.

If someone is sabotaging what you are doing, it's not necessarily because they're being malicious. It may be because they have an unconscious investment in keeping you the same. Nobody likes change. We all want to know what is going to happen. We all want to feel that we have some familiarity with those we love and with what is going on around us. You not only have to explore your feelings and investments, but you need to take a look at the primary relationships around you. You're not going through this process alone. Everyone is involved! For example, if you get a very different response from a person each time you go up to them, you are going to feel quite wary about approaching them. If they're quite friendly on one occasion, but bite your head off the next time you see them, you will feel very uneasy and unsure. People like to feel they can count on things being the same. So if you start changing your act, you need to take the people in your life through the process with you. It will help them understand what you are trying to do and it will be less threatening to them.

Goals

An area that people are often vague about is what their life goals are. How do you expect to know where you are going, how you're going

NOW THAT I HAVE THESE HABITS

to get there or what you've achieved if you don't even know what your goals are in the first place? This is one way in which people sabotage themselves. You need to begin to prioritise your life. We want to make the best possible use of our energy and time. And believe me, personal growth takes both.

Take time to think about what is important to you. What are you willing to do to achieve your goals? Make sure that they are realistic. You want to programme in success. But don't be afraid to be expansive either. Make yourself a list of short-term goals and long-term goals (one month, six months, one year, five years, ten years). Go over them on a regular basis. See what you have achieved. Keep adding to them and revising as needed. Making a list does help the unconscious mind to pick up the idea and begin to act upon it. Write your goals in the first person and keep them in the present tense, whatever the timespan involved. For example:

6 months
- I feel good about my body.

1 year
- I am free from compulsive eating.

5 years
- I make £30,000 a year!

You should include career goals as well as personal goals.

You have to be very conscious about what is going on in your mind in order to break the cycle of compulsive eating before it starts. You have to know what you're feeling. You need to think before you put food in your mouth. Right now, it's still just a hand-to-mouth, automatic motion. You're not thinking about what you're doing. And sometimes rightly so, because you *want* to overeat and if you think about it, you might not! This is where your priorities come into play. What do you really want?

HOMEWORK

PRACTICAL STEPS

Below is a mental checklist that you should go through every time you want to eat. You may even want to put this up on your refrigerator.

Ask yourself:
- How am I feeling?
- What do I want?
- Will food give me what I want?
- What are the consequences? Will it be worth it?

If you then choose to eat, fine. But you need to give yourself the benefit of a conscious choice.

WRITTEN EXERCISES

1 What patterns did you develop to survive your family? Did they get you what you wanted, did they work for you? Are they still working for you?

2 Make a list of the behaviour you don't want to continue.

Write out what your investment in continuing each form of behaviour is, and what you would get out of not continuing it. Then make a decision about whether or not you want to work on changing this behaviour. The questions below will help you get started:

- What do you get out of compulsive eating? What would happen if you didn't eat compulsively?

- What does overeating do for you? Does it make you happy?
  What reinforces your compulsive eating? What would be your reasons for changing your eating patterns?

- Do you really want to eat consciously? Is it safer to stay where you are?

- What are you willing to do in order to make some changes? Are you willing to go through some emotional discomfort?

9

PRACTICAL INFORMATION ABOUT FOOD AND HOW IT CAN CREATE EATING DIFFICULTIES

I t is pointless to talk about calories *per se*. I'm sure that you're all too aware of the calorie content of most foods. In fact, I'm sure you could probably give me the calorie content of this piece of paper! But you don't need to count calories in order to recover from compulsive eating. It's not necessary, in fact, it will work against you. It will put you back into the dieter's mentality that you need to forget forever!

It is important, however, to understand the dynamic between what is eaten and how it is utilised in your body. You need to find out what your body needs to keep it functioning and healthy. Some of the primary causes of disease have to do with what we put in our bodies. I know that may sound a bit simplistic, but it is true. Food is extremely powerful in terms of our well-being, our ability to function and our emotional equanimity. The body is an amazing piece of machinery and it can take quite a bit of abuse, but it will also produce immediate or chronic difficulties if what we require it to assimilate is entirely inappropriate to its needs.

There are so many books written on health that it's hard to know what to believe. What is the proper way to eat for maximum health? Do we need vitamin supplements? Is it possible to eat healthy foods and feel satisfied? We'll explore these questions, and you'll find additional reading material in the Resources section.

Do you even care about being healthy? I was willing to sacrifice health for slimness, but now I know that being slim isn't any fun if you're not well enough to enjoy it!

Allergies and food sensitivities

Sometimes we crave things that we are actually allergic to. There are numerous symptoms that can point to these food sensitivities. They include sudden mood swings, headaches, migraines, irritable bowel syndrome, digestive problems, premenstrual tension, skin conditions and recurrent infections. Often people who have food allergies have a long list of vague symptoms and most GPs don't know what to do with these woolly complaints. However, it is precisely these ill-defined symptoms that can mean there is something wrong with what you are eating. You don't have to have itchy eyes or break out in hives to discover that you are allergic (or addicted) to certain foods and conditions, so watch out for any symptoms you might have.

Food intolerances affect us physically and emotionally. They also influence our temperament and our ability to think clearly. There have been plenty of scientific studies pointing to difficult behaviour and hyperactivity in children as a result of particular flavourings and colourings in foods. These affect adults as well. Certain colourings have even been taken off the market because of the adverse effects they have on people. And what's interesting about sensitivities is that you only have to ingest a minute amount of the offending substance to elicit a full-blown reaction. It also takes about seventy-two hours for a substance to dissipate completely and to leave the body each time you eat it. So you may have to live with some residual affects for a couple of days.

I remember one summer in college while rehearsing for a musical I was taking part in. As usual, I was dieting, not eating much one day, then eating too much the next. Starve, binge, starve, binge. You know the cycle. I had gone to the rehearsal on an empty stomach, not having eaten since the night before. We rehearsed all day and were going to take a dinner break early in the evening, then return and work some more. My voice was feeling a bit rough and I had more singing to do, so I went to a chemist during the break to get some cough mixture to soothe my throat. I bought some cough syrup whose only ingredients were listed as being honey and lemon. It tasted quite nice and felt very smooth going down my throat. But being a person who can't do anything in moderation, I continued to sip the mixture until most of the bottle was gone.

Back in the rehearsal, some strange things started to happen. Everything seemed to go into slow motion. My thoughts got completely confused and I couldn't remember my directions from one moment to the next. My speech was slow and slurred. My director had to stop rehearsals, and I was led away in tears. 'What's happening to me?' I thought. I felt as though I wasn't in control of my body. My director said that my eyes were glazed over as if I were drunk. I felt as if I had been drugged. I started to crave protein, which is a natural antidote to sugar, so I had some and finally began to feel more normal again. Had I known about my sensitivity to honey, I could have avoided this whole incident. It was one of the scariest things that ever happened to me.

Food sensitivities can also interfere with the metabolic process and with the production of insulin. Some overweight people don't always produce the insulin necessary to keep their blood sugar at a balanced level. This causes the blood sugar to rise, fat to be deposited and not used up and the desire for more food. So in essence, people get thrown into another kind of vicious cycle, looking for food to maintain their energy because what was put in before hasn't been utilised properly and is now accumulating as fat.

ELIMINATE THE PROBLEM

In this day and age, people are becoming more sensitive to the environment and all the pollutants within it. More and more people are developing sensitivities to the flavourings, additives and chemicals in our food supply. We are eating less and less fresh, unprocessed food. In some ways, we're helping to make ourselves feel ill with what we eat. There's no need to suffer like this. If you had frequent migraines and you found out that eating cheese caused these, you would probably be happy to stop eating cheese for a while to save yourself such distress. Similarly, if you suspect that you might be sensitive to a certain food, eliminate it from your diet for anything from a week to a month. When you reintroduce it, notice what, if any, effect it has on you. Eliminating foods that you are sensitive to doesn't mean that you have to do without them for the rest of your life. Often just refraining from eating certain foods for a few months is sufficient to desensitise you, though you may have to be careful about how frequently you continue to eat the item.

There is a test called the 'vega test' which can determine whether you have any allergies or food sensitivities. It's not very expensive, about £25 or £30, and it takes about forty-five minutes. It can also indicate if you have any vitamin or mineral deficiencies. It's much faster than the old allergy testing methods or strict elimination diets, and there is no discomfort involved. If you are interested in this test, I have included relevant information in the Resources section. There are other methods of testing for sensitivities. You can ask at health-food stores or alternative healing centres to find out if they are able to offer tests. My feeling is that the more you know about your body, the more you can learn to work with it and the less you will sabotage yourself unwittingly. Knowing your sensitivities can also help eliminate unnecessary discomfort.

I have one client who is aware that whenever she eats anything with wheat or yeast in it, she immediately gets bloated. Being bloated isn't normal. If you bloat up after eating, it means one of three things. Either you ate a food that you are sensitive to, or you ate some poor combinations that make digestion slow and difficult, or you ate much more than your body can process in the usual amount of time. The same goes for flatulence, indigestion or heartburn. Those are not the body's natural responses. They mean your body is trying to tell you that something is out of balance! It's not that your body is trying to give you a hard time, it's just trying to help you right yourself.

You might also want to observe how you feel in general, physically and emotionally. See if you can make any connections between certain foods and certain physical or emotional states. Most people put so many different kinds of food and drink and pollutants in their bodies that it's impossible to sort out what made them feel a certain way on any given day.

Addictive foods

The body wants to eat real food. That's why when you eat junk food, you don't feel satisfied. The body keeps looking for more. And some foods are actually addictive. Cravings to addictive food substances like chocolate, sugar, caffeine, etc. are never satisfied. You can eat them non-stop, but your body will look for more because they are designed to create desire not diminish it. If you crave an addictive substance, it's simply because it's addictive and not because your body needs it.

There are reasons why we seem to be addicted to some foods. This can be explained by the release of **endorphins**, hormones, and **exorphins**, which are proteins that have an effect similar to opium. Some food products contain these chemicals. When food is digested properly, everything gets broken down and there is no effect on the nervous system. However, if it doesn't get broken down and these products enter the bloodstream, they can produce a state that is very similar to taking an addictive drug. Something similar happens when people starve themselves: chemical changes occur in the brain, endorphins are released and they feel a sense of euphoria. This makes starving oneself a very appealing idea.

Chocolate is the food most often cited when discussing food

addictions. People, particularly women, seem to crave it when they are depressed or just before they start their periods. Many people find it so alluring that they call themselves chocaholics. Again, there are chemical reasons for this desire. It has a mood-altering chemical in it called beta phenylethylamine, which acts very much like an amphetamine. It also contains caffeine and theobromine, which are both stimulants. No wonder we crave it when we are feeling a bit down. The body knows that it will give us a lift! (Remember the body has a memory, too.)

I used to be included in the chocaholic hall of fame as well. The way I stopped was by giving it up altogether and substituting carob for it. I don't miss chocolate, and I don't get any repercussions from carob. Some of the things that can help you kick chocolate are:

- eat some protein when you crave something sweet;
- don't drink things with caffeine in them;
- look for carob or other non-sugar treats.
- And if you don't want to experiment with giving up chocolate; don't try. You don't have to do anything you don't want!

How to decipher cravings

Not all cravings are detrimental or suspect. If you pay attention, your body will give you a lot of answers. There is an easy way to determine if you need what you are craving. If you crave something and you eat it and your body goes 'Ah' and feels satisfied, then you know that you probably needed to eat that food for some physical reason. If you crave something and you eat it and your body says, 'Wow, where can I get more, I just have to have more, how soon can I get it, how much can I consume immediately?', then I would certainly suspect that there is something else going on. Addictive cravings never get satisfied!

A good exercise is to take a piece of paper and draw a line down the middle. On the left-hand side write down all the foods you really like, the foods you are most likely to want to overeat, the foods that you consider forbidden or bad. On the right-hand side of the sheet, write down the foods that you crave most often. Then compare the two columns. Find any correlations? Don't be surprised if a lot of foods appear in both columns. The important thing is not to sabotage yourself with foods that you are addicted to.

A woman I met recently told me that she went through packets of peppermints on a daily basis. She told me that she couldn't pass a petrol station or a shop without going in to buy some. She ate them all day long. I asked her if she was craving the sugar or the peppermint. She said she didn't have a clue. The next time I saw her, she said she had done an experiment. She bought herself some oil of peppermint in a health-food shop. And instead of eating mints, she would put some of this oil on her tongue whenever she craved the mints. To her surprise, she didn't miss the sugar one bit and was quite happy to have the pure peppermint. This one small experiment not only saved her money but also a great deal of unnecessary sugar consumption.

Sometimes it seems there is so much working against us! Compulsive eating is a complex matter. That is why you must recognise the potential limits in each area: physical, emotional and psychological. You must be clever about the food choices that you make. Not because they may be fattening, but because of the overall effect. You must become conscious of your eating patterns. And you must learn how to cope with what you feel as well as be able to express it in ways that are positive for you.

Sugar

There is an innate preference in humans for the taste of sweet things. In studies between 1973 and 1982, it was discovered that even newborns prefer the taste of sugar solutions to water and even to formula baby foods. Researchers reckon that it has to do with the sweet taste eliciting a feeling of safety and also that it's a survival instinct, because sweet things are generally high in calories.

Humans originally developed a sweet tooth with natural sugars like fruit, but today we are more likely to satisfy this desire with processed, packaged junk foods. It seems that, in the West where food is abundant, we have moved from an instinctual response for survival to an addictive one, because people are looking for palatability in food rather than nourishment. Having lived most of my life in America, I can tell you that the amount of junk food and 'non-food' that is eaten there is astounding. On the other hand, the British consume the largest amount of sugar per person in the world!

> ❧ *Just over 200 years ago, we used to take four or five pounds of sugar (about two kilograms) a year; by the middle of the nineteenth century, this had increased five-fold to about twenty-five pounds a year; we now take about a hundred pounds a year.'* ❧
>
> [From *Pure, White and Deadly* by John Yudkin]

I have always been addicted and sensitive to sugar, but for many years I didn't realise this. When I was a teenager, I often couldn't go to sleep at night unless I had a final snack. I'm not sure if this was something I decided I needed emotionally or if it was an actual physical requirement. I would often make a late-night trip to the kitchen when no one else was around for my sugar nightcap. One night, I knew there was a fresh cake in the house. We always had plenty of fresh pastry, candy, biscuits and ice-cream stored in our two freezers and refrigerator. Anyway, this cake was waiting for me on the worktop. I loved the sugary icing, but was never all that keen on the actual sponge. I ran my finger around the rim and licked it. It was so good and sweet that I did it again. But I had started something that I couldn't stop. I continued to take bits of icing off the cake until I had removed a good-size piece. So I cut off the naked cake and threw it away. But I still couldn't stop myself. I continued around the cake, picking off more and more of the icing and then slicing off the cake underneath and throwing it away. I realised that what I was doing was not at all normal, but I couldn't stop myself. I ate more and more icing until I had removed all of it, but there still was some cake that I hadn't thrown out. I was in such a dilemma. I knew that I couldn't just bin the other half of the cake, or my mother would wonder how a whole cake disappeared while everyone slept. But I also knew that it would be obvious that I had done it if I left the remainder of the cake sitting there without any icing on it. I just went to bed in a complete state hoping that somehow it wouldn't matter in the morning. Of course, the next morning my mother discovered the cake, and I was completely humiliated. I felt totally out of control, and it didn't take long before the whole family knew what I had done. I thought that my desire and inability to stay away from it had to do with some inadequacy within myself. I didn't realise that it was an addictive substance and I was particularly sensitive to it.

THE DEVIL IN DISGUISE

There is absolutely nothing positive to be said about sugar other than it tastes good. It tampers with the body's use of proteins. It interferes with digestion and causes fermentation in the stomach, making your food petrify instead of process. It can create heartburn and indigestion. It is associated with ulcers, dental disease, diabetes and coronary disease, to name a few. And it provokes an enlargement of the liver and kidneys. Sounds terrific so far, doesn't it!

Sugar has no nutritional value whatsoever. It simply adds calories and sets up cravings for more. And it is in practically everything that is processed. It is difficult to find packaged foods that don't have any sugar in them. It's even in most toothpastes! Manufacturers aren't stupid. They know that including it, even in small amounts, will make you want to come back for more of whatever product it's in. So beware of labelling. Anything that has '-ose' on the end (like sucrose, maltose, fructose, lactose, dextrose) is a form of sugar. If you are sensitive to sugar or if you crave it a lot, you may be sabotaging yourself by eating hidden sugar. You may think that you just don't have any control over your eating when, in fact, it may just be that you've eaten something laced with sugar.

I discovered a book called *Sugar Blues* by William Duffy in the late 1970s. In it, he describes the history of sugar, its chemical make-up and how it's utilised in the body. I was so convinced I needed to experiment with giving it up, that I did. I checked everything in my cupboards and threw away anything with any hint of sugar in it. I found that when I stopped eating sugar, my binge episodes were reduced by about ninety percent. I also gave up honey at the same time. This was one of the most helpful things I have ever done in my life.

The first time I gave up eating sugar was for about seven years. And in case you're interested, those were also my thinnest years. Later on, when I started to add it back in again, I noticed that it made me tired and cranky. It led to a host of nasty symptoms that I would never have been able to understand had I not stayed away from it. When I was diagnosed as having intestinal **candida**, I realised why. Sugar is one of the substances that feeds the candida. So I still only eat sugar extremely rarely. But I don't feel deprived – it's not worth the trouble that it causes me! There are many ways to make foods sweet without having to resort to sugar. You can use juice concentrates or brown rice syrup to make sweet treats. These can all be found in health-food shops.

Felicity had been working with me for about a month when she succumbed to a binge lasting the better part of a weekend. When she came into my office, she was tearful and tired and depressed. She felt that all the good work and progress that she had been making had been erased by this one event. When we started talking about what had precipitated the overeating, she was readily able to put her finger on the provocation. She had been feeling lonely and fat and she had some social invitations for the weekend. To ease her rising anxiety over having to get dressed up and go out, she ate something sugary. Well, that was the last she saw of any peace of mind for three days. The sugar kicked off the desire for more and she stopped listening to the nurturing part of herself. She ate without discretion and without giving herself the chance to make any conscious choices. She ate things just because they were there and she was feeling low. At some point, she was able to take stock of what she was doing and she stopped eating sugar. But it did take a few days for the 'sugar blues' to wear off and she was still in the midst of them when I saw her. Before this incident, she had never made the connection between sugar and its effect on her emotional state. But after this particular weekend of eating, she noticed how much more exaggerated the sugar made her depression and anxiety. Felicity has now realised that it's best for her to make sensible choices about when and how to eat sugar. For instance, if she wants a piece of cake, she goes out and buys only one piece. She doesn't bring home boxes of sugary things to torture herself with. She has also discovered that sugar has much less impact on her emotionally if she eats it after a decent meal.

I could list you countless clients who have reduced their overeating and lost weight simply by taking sugar out of their daily eating. If you have a tendency to crave sweets, you may want to experiment with removing sugar, or eating it only when outside your home. I know this isn't an easy thing to do, but I also know that the craving continues if you feed it and it goes away if you don't. But again, the first principle is to feel that you can eat whatever you like. You must get past this deprivation idea before you can move on to experimenting with giving up certain foods. Wait until you are ready and want to do so. You will never be relaxed with food until you feel that you are making choices about what you eat because you want to, not because you think you should!

Food combining and digestion

This is an area which might help you a lot. You have probably already heard about food combining or the Hay diet. This is not a new concept. Dr Hay was born in Pennsylvania, USA, in 1866. He developed some serious difficulties with his health and no one seemed to have any answers for him, except to tell him to make sure his affairs were in order. Like myself, Dr Hay used his own body as a laboratory. He began experimenting and came up with a system for eating that he hoped would make a difference. His experiments certainly accomplished that and much more. He restored himself to a state of health and he began helping others.

He also found that people who ate foods combined in a certain way didn't become overweight. This wasn't because they eliminated all the tasty foods in life, it had to do with the body assimilating foods more effectively and effortlessly. The idea of food combining is to make digestion an easy and simple process for the body. I became interested in food combining for that reason, as my digestion has always been sluggish. Proper combining does increase nutrition and energy levels. The digestive tract works best if it has little demand placed upon it.

Different foods require different **enzymes** to digest them. They take different amounts of time to break down in the stomach. Fruits remain in the stomach an hour or less. Starches are in the stomach for two to three hours, proteins for about four hours. Complex foods like beans (which are a mixture of carbohydrate and protein) can remain in the stomach for five to six hours. These are the estimates if the food is eaten alone. Start combining the foods, and it takes much longer to process them. Low-fibre foods take about forty-eight hours to process completely through the body, as opposed to high-fibre foods, which take sixteen to twenty-four hours. In Africa, people's food goes completely through their system from mouth to waste in about twenty-four hours. In the West, we take from two to four days to do the same job. So you can see that you are asking your body to do a lot of work just for each meal! It makes sense that people are often tired after eating. The body has too much to try and sort out. If it has to use all its resources to process what you've put in it, it doesn't have any energy left over for you to do other things!

PROBLEM AREAS

Certain condiments inhibit digestion. Drinking liquids before, during or right after eating also slows down the digestive process, as it dilutes your digestive juices. Fats tend to coat other food in the stomach, preventing the digestive enzymes access to it. This is one of the reasons why people have some milk or cream before they drink alcohol. The fat coats the stomach, so the alcohol is not absorbed into the bloodstream so quickly.

Some combinations of foods produce fermentation in your stomach. If this acid condition is present, then there isn't much in the way of processing and assimilation going on. The fermentation comes from putting foods that take a long time to digest in first and then throwing down something like fruit that wants to just whiz through, but can't because there are other things in the way. This fermentation can cause heartburn. This is a sign of poor food combining, as there's a fight going on in your stomach. Indigestion, burping, sleeplessness, flatulence and feeling bloated after eating can all be signs of poor food combining.

The basic rule in food combining is that you don't eat protein and starch together at the same time. You only eat foods that are compatible. You can combine proteins with fruit or proteins with vegetables. Or you can combine fruit and vegetables with starches. But you wouldn't combine, say, cheese and bread. This is the part that usually gets to people! Most people eat sandwiches as a mainstay for their midday meal. You can still eat sandwiches and follow food combining, but you could only fill the sandwich with avocado or vegetables. Avocado is the one food that you can put with anything; vegetables, starch, fruit or other protein. It is suggested that milk should be taken by itself and that wine and cider shouldn't be mixed with ale or beer, though you can mix whisky or gin with either. If you would like to explore further, the best book that I have found on the subject is called *Food Combining For Health* by Grant and Joice. However, only look into food combining if it's something that interests you. You don't have to do it to recover from compulsive eating. And you certainly don't want to try it if you still feel deprived around food.

The body has a rhythmic cycle

If you eat all day long, there isn't time for the food to be processed. Some of it sits in the stomach putrefying. Some is moved into the intestines to make room for the additional food coming into the stomach, even though it hasn't been broken down properly. Your muscles get tired, food jams up, and constipation can be one of the results. Overloading your system can cause enervation and **toxaemia** (blood poisoning). You can also begin to see that some food is never utilised for nutrition and instead becomes waste for storage. It's amazing just how important digestion is to the maintenance of health and weight.

The body has a natural rhythm for all its processes. From 4 a.m. until noon is the time for getting rid of the waste that has accumulated. Later in the morning, the digestive process begins to peak (usually around noon). This is one reason why it's good to eat your largest meal of the day at this time, because the body is more able to process it then. From about noon until 8 p.m., the body concerns itself with eating and digestion. But the body doesn't want to be digesting while it is resting. From 8 p.m. until 4 a.m. is the body's time for rest and assimilation. So it's best to have finished eating for the day before it gets too late. Often that midnight snack could be stagnating in your stomach or disturbing your sleep.

Digestion begins in the mouth. Your saliva and teeth start the process. This is one of the reasons you were told to chew your food properly. You weren't being nagged just for the fun of it! Carbohydrates in particular begin to be digested in the mouth. Each part of your body has its part to play in turning food into energy or waste. You want your food to be already broken down so the stomach can then do its part when it arrives. Eat chewy foods, food that takes a while to break down. This gives the digestive enzymes in your mouth a chance to help. You will find chewing a satisfying experience, because you will feel as if you have just eaten something. Chewy foods also tend to provide bulk for your intestines.

A chain reaction begins every time you put something into your mouth. Problems can occur anywhere along the way if the previous organ has not been able to do its job properly. It's also a good idea always to sit down when eating. Relaxing and eating slowly will aid your digestion. And remember that a lot of overeating occurs when people are on the run or they are unconscious about what they are doing.

HOMEWORK

PRACTICAL STEPS

- Begin to experiment with foods. Try to eat very simple meals that don't combine a lot of different foods in one sitting. (You're not dieting or restricting your intake! This is to find out if any foods affect you in a negative way.) If you feel like you are dieting, then stop the experiment.

- Begin to notice how you feel physically after eating, or after eating certain foods.

- If you feel you are ready, try eliminating sugar or chocolate from your diet for one week, then eat it again and see how you feel.

WRITTEN EXERCISES

1 What kinds of foods do you eat together?

2 Have you noticed any times when food just seems to sit in your stomach? When are those times? Can you associate it with specific types of foods?

3 What kinds of foods do you crave? Is there a particular time of the day or month that you crave it?

4 What have you noticed about eating foods that you crave?

5 Do you have any of these symptoms: generally low energy, sluggish digestion, headaches, constipation? What symptoms do you have?

10

EATING TO MATCH YOUR BODY TYPE

I n chapter 1 I talked about body types, and we will look at the subject in more detail in this section.

Heredity

Let's talk about fat itself. Do you think you're overweight? Has anyone told you that you need to lose weight? If they have, was this for reasons of their own preference or was it an objective statement? Given the social pressure for women to be thinner than what is realistic, it is not always easy to determine if you're the weight that is actually right for you. Finding your ideal weight should be based on genetics and body type, not on personal or public opinion.

Even the height and weight tables that are published can only be used to give us the basic parameters. Your body type and genetics contribute to what your optimum weight should be. Some good questions to guide you to your ideal weight are:

- At what weight do I feel healthy?
- At this weight, do I feel able to move my body around comfortably?

- Do I feel confident emotionally about my body?
- At this weight, are there 'extra bits' drooping or wiggling that get in my way?
- Extra bits may be a sign of age or lack of tone and not necessarily fat.

Sometimes we may not like our genetically determined shape. But fighting against genetics can be as fruitless as dieting. This is why it's terribly important that you take a look around your family. What do the rest of your family members look like? What do you grandparents look like? What characteristics have they passed along to you? Unfortunately, if your heritage is of hefty people, then you may never be able to become a small person. At least, not happily or naturally. So if this is the case, you would be much better off accepting your size and forgetting about trying to alter your body.

Haskew and Adams (*When Food Is a Four-Letter Word*) list the top two risk factors for becoming overweight as an adult as being female and having parent(s)/grandparent(s) who were obese. Some statistics indicate that, if you have one parent who is obese, then you have a forty-percent chance of becoming an obese adult. And if both parents are obese, you have an eighty-percent chance of becoming obese. If you have any of these factors in place, don't despair quite yet – there are many other factors that contribute significantly to becoming overweight. As I have stated before, it's as complex as the individual. Socio-economic status, race, ethnic origins, stress, learned behaviours and dieting all play a part in determining a person's size.

Zoë is an example of someone with genetic predisposition towards obesity that didn't sentence her to a life as a fatty. Zoë's grandparents on both sides came from English and European farming stock. These were people who lived in a cool climate and worked outside a great deal of their time, attending to livestock and running their farms. They ate and worked heartily. The women tended to be quite round and the men quite square. Neither set of grandparents was particularly tall. Neither of her grandmothers would fit the current description of having fashionable figures. Zoë's mother is smaller than her maternal grandmother, but her shape is pretty much the same. Her mother lived life on the farm until she was about seventeen, when she moved to England. Zoë's father is taller than his own father and, in his middle-age, began to get something of a bulge around his middle. He is stocky but not particularly flabby. Both of Zoë's parents lived through the rationing of the Second World War, although this had ceased by the time Zoë was born.

Food in their household was simple and unfussy. They didn't eat a lot of creamy sauces or sweets, and food wasn't used as consolation for emotional upsets (at least her parents did not offer them to Zoë when she was distressed). But as Zoë got older, she took it upon herself to use sweets and junk foods for solace. This, of course, began to add extra pounds on her body, so she began dieting to relieve herself of them. The dieting only made matters worse. It made her feel as if she had to eat differently from her parents. It made her all the more apt to eat secretly, and the sugary treats often led to binges.

So, could we say that she became overweight because of her genetic structure? No. Certainly she came from a lineage of people who were not particularly slender, but her weight actually came more from her use of food during emotional upheaval. In turn, the dieting made her behaviour around food more erratic and made her weight fluctuate even more. Genetics do play an important part in predisposing a person to weight problems, but people must also be responsible for how they use what they have.

In case you are wondering, both of my grandmothers were large, round people. My grandfathers were pretty average in size. My father was very stocky and solid; he was large, but not tall or flabby. He always kept an eye on his weight and underate a lot throughout his adult life. My mother is medium height and basically on the round end of average. She dieted into her fifties and then gave up. Her weight has continued to rise with age. I have my father's wide ribcage and my mother's long torso with short legs. My tendency as a child was to be chubby. I didn't really allow myself to wait and see what the tail-end of puberty would bring me as a figure, because I started to manipulate it early on and continued into adulthood. I've had so many figures that I didn't stop long enough to attribute any of them to genetics, though the basic structure is quite similar to my parents.

Body types

Your body type plays an important role in what your optimum weight will be, as well as your genetic heritage. There are three basic body types. They are the endomorph, mesomorph and ectomorph. Each body type also has certain physical and emotional characteristics that accompany it. People are not always just one body type – they can be a combination of two – but there is usually one structure that predominates.

ENDOMORPHS

The **endomorphic** body type reveals itself in a sturdy frame, usually not too tall. The body tends to be kind of meaty and the features round. The weight of people with this type of body structure often fluctuates more than other body types. They are typically those who carry extra weight. This isn't just because of the physical structure of their bodies but because of certain personality characteristics that seem to go along with each body type. We will explore those in a moment.

An endomorphic body, when in fine condition, can also be very athletic. It's a shapely body with developed muscles or curves. Rubens' women tend to be endomorphic types, as are those men that we call 'macho' or 'jocks'. The Queen has an endormorphic body, and so do Raquel Welsh and Tom Cruise. So you can see that they can look quite different, even though the body type is the same. (In case you're wondering, I have an endomorphic body.)

Endomorphic body type

Mesomorphic body type

Ectomorphic body type

MESOMORPHS

The **mesomorphic** body type tends to be pretty stable. People with this body type can be quite tall and angular in shape, but they don't usually have a problem with their weight fluctuating. Their bodies can be somewhat underdeveloped in terms of broad chests (for men) or fuller breasts (for women). Some women with this particular body type tend to have what we would call 'little boy' figures. These are often the people who claim, 'Oh, I just tried on my wedding dress from twenty years ago and it still fits!' Prince Charles has this type of body.

ECTOMORPHS

The **ectomorphic** body is the type that we love to hate. Ecto-morphs are the people who tend to be underweight, if anything. They can be either small, petite and fragile, or tall, slender model types. For men, they can sometimes be described as the 'ninety-pound weakling' variety. Ectomorphic body types are also able to eat pretty much whatever they want, whenever they want and not gain weight. In fact, they are often the ones we hear moaning that they can't seem to gain weight no matter what they do. Twiggy, Kate Moss and Mick Jagger have this type of body.

You probably thought there was a lot more variation in bodies. Take a look around you. What type of body do you have? Are you a combination? What type of body structures do your family members have? It's important to take a realistic look at what your body type is because you can't change the basic bone structure of your body. If you're short, you can't expect to look like a long-legged ballerina, even if you lose weight. It's just not possible! Yet we are given so many messages about what to expect when we've lost weight that we often think the impossible is probable. Being realistic about yourself is vital to relax yourself out of compulsive eating. We are working with real feelings, real bodies and real possibilities, not fantasies.

What size and shape do you want to be? Is it reasonable, given the body type you have? Do you even know what your body actually looks like? Body-image distortion is very common for chronic dieters and compulsive eaters. We often see ourselves as larger or smaller than we actually are. Photographs are not a very good gauge because the camera tends to add pounds and also the angle and lighting on any given photo can make you look very different. It can be very deceptive. You'll also tend to be more confused about your actual size if your weight has fluctuated a lot over the years. If you don't feel sure about what you look like, try the following exercise.

- Take a large piece of newspaper roll (if you can get some), or shelf- or wall-lining paper, or piece together some large sheets of paper.
- Lie down on the paper and ask a friend to take a marker pen and draw around your body. Ask them to draw as close to your body as they can (you want this to be as realistic as possible).
- Then cut out the outline and tack it up on your wall so you can take a good look at it.

This is an exercise you may wish to repeat about once a year to get a realistic image of what your body looks like.

When I was going through my anorexic phase, I typically thought of myself as much larger than was actually the case. One of the things I tried in order to get a grip on my size was to ask a friend whom I considered quite petite to try on a pair of my jeans. I felt stupid asking her to do it, but she was happy to oblige. In my mind's eye, I was much larger than she was, even though (at the time) we wore the same size. When she tried on my jeans, I couldn't believe my eyes. They fitted her perfectly. Just as they fitted me. They weren't too large or too small. So I had to start believing that I was indeed a small person!

Personalities that match the body

Let's move on to the personality characteristics that go with each body type.

ENDOMORPHS

Endomorphs are vital, energetic people. They are creative and good self-starters. They can have great spurts of energy and attention for projects, but find it difficult to sustain their interest. They often put out a great deal of energy and then have to shut down to recover, though they do recuperate quickly. Endomorphs don't like to co-operate with their bodies and are weak in self-discipline. The endomorphic body doesn't usually get enough rest or exercise. They can be very impulsive and overly sensitive. They also might be easy to anger or have explosive tempers, but their anger probably dissipates quickly. The endomorph's most prominent emotional disposition is that of anger, whether it's suppressed or expressed. This isn't to say that they go around angry all the time, but it's their most frequent emotional reaction. A lot of endomorphs would like to believe that they are happy-go-lucky and don't feel that it is acceptable to get angry, so anger often subtly builds up inside. They can often rationalise themselves out of feeling angry.

This body type relates to the world in very physical terms. They feel the world and their participation in it through their bodies. They can be very sensual or athletic. They enjoy indulging in the pleasures of the body: food, sex, alcohol and perhaps even drugs (even tending to misuse stimulants). Because of this, they tend to become toxic easily. Not having very strong elimination systems, they often store a lot of emotional energy or waste in the body. The endomorph has very little patience for any physical discomfort; they don't like to feel uncomfortable and want to rid themselves of any uneasiness as soon as possible. Because they identify so heavily with the body, they may get physically ill from an emotional upset.

MESOMORPHS

The mesomorphs can be very rational in their approach to life. They tend to be the stoics, the unwavering, the analytical. To them, the brain is superior to the body. They try to control their lives through the use of their mental faculties and may get quite upset if they feel they are not in control. They don't like chaos; they like things to be orderly and to go as planned. These are not the most spontaneous of people. On the other hand, though, they are probably very reliable and responsible. They may find it difficult to get in touch with their emotions, and one reason is because they don't see the value of being emotional. They don't like emotional displays from themselves or others. You wouldn't be able to convince a mesomorph of anything if you were hysterical in your approach. But if you stay cool, calm and collected, you will gain their attention.

The mesomorph's primary emotional response to life is fear. They are fearful of life in general and are reserved and careful in making judgements or taking risks. They may not feel themselves as fearful but rather as cautious. But it's their fear of lack of control that stops them. These are the people who won't allow themselves to get too excited about potential situations in case they fall through. These are the types of people who can wait until their birthday morning to open a package that arrives for them a week early. As children, they probably had a savings account or at least didn't spend their pocket money all in one go! These people would never consider eating their pudding before their main course! They may not be very in touch with the desires of the body because their minds often override their physical wants or needs.

ECTOMORPHS

The ectomorph is a person who doesn't want to have to deal with the practical realities of living. They can be quite romantic and dreamlike. They override the mind with their emotions; they aren't terribly interested in even *being* in a body. And because of this, they can be very dissociated from their body and its needs. These are often the people who forget to eat (if you can imagine that being possible!). They can be the 'absent-minded professor types' or the artistic, melancholy types. Their bodies, as well as their presentation, can be light and airy. They find that most things in life are an emotional dilemma for them and they hate anything coming to an end. They always seem to be confused about having to make decisions. Decisions can take forever, and often they don't make them at all. They get very bogged down in detail and have difficulty seeing the whole picture. These people frequently don't finish what they've started because they feel they can't cope with it. This is different from endomorphs, who don't finish projects because they've simply lost interest.

The ectomorph can get fairly hysterical. They can shut themselves off from their feelings by remaining confused. They don't always understand that there is a distinct difference between being emotional and feeling their feelings. When you uncover their emotional reaction to life, their primary state is sorrow. But in their defence, the ectomorph is most likely to be the person who is happy and willing to listen to your feelings. They can be very good at nurturing others.

Remember, people are not necessarily just one body type or temperament, but are more likely to be a combination. However, one type will probably be predominant. In my experience working with eating disorders, I've noticed that compulsive overeaters tend to be endomorphs, anorexics tend to be mesomorphs and bulimics tend to be ectomorphs or ectomorph/mesomorph combinations. Of course this is something of a generalisation, but it has been very interesting to see the connections.

Food use and body types

ENDOMORPHS

The endomorphic body type is already quite grounded to earth. They feel rooted in the body. They therefore don't need to eat a lot of foods; a low-carbohydrate diet suits them the best. They also don't need foods that are concentrated or acidic. They should be careful about salt and dairy products, as they will function better without these. The person with the endomorphic body type will feel better on a diet that has a high percentage of raw foods (fruits and vegetables). They want to watch their consumption of things that toxify the body, like red meats and alcohol. They need to make sure they get enough vitamins A and D; this can be accomplished through sunflower seeds and sunlight.

In my own case, for example, I have difficulty digesting pulses and grains. They just seem too heavy for my system. When I eat them, I feel quite full and generally I feel tired, lethargic and dull. This is partly due to the fact that they do take a lot of time to digest in any body and partly due to my body's idiosyncrasies. By now you know enough about how I operate to guess that I don't eat pulses and grains very much! I like to feel good after eating, not sluggish.

MESOMORPHS

The mesomorphic body type doesn't have to use food in quite the same way as the other two. It doesn't seem to have such a struggle one way or the other with certain foods. This body type can eat a balance between the more earthy and light foods. But even mesomorphs can become toxic or enervated if they overwork their digestion.

ECTOMORPHS

The ectomorphic body type is quite different. These people feel quite airy. Because of this, they should limit their intake of fruit; it's too light for them. They're not grounded by their bodies, so they need to eat food that will help do that for them. They will find themselves better able to concentrate by eating more grains, potatoes and cooked foods. Their deficiencies tend to show up in their nervous systems, and therefore they should take care to have enough niacin, calcium and magnesium. They also need to look out for the B vitamins.

Help yourself by becoming familiar with who you are and what you need. You deserve to be successful, but you may be working against yourself and not knowing it. There is no reason to make recovery from compulsive eating any more difficult than it already has been! The more you feed your body the things that it actually needs, the happier you will find yourself emotionally. What people put into their bodies affects more than just the physical aspect of well-being. One thing I have noticed is that I seem to eat almost exactly the same amount of food every day, with slight variations. I think if someone followed me around with a calculator and added up everything that I ate, it would be very close each day. This is not because I plan it, this is just what my body asks for.

Adapt to your circumstances

Being attentive to your physical patterns can relieve you of much undue stress. There may be a good reason why you are experiencing an increase or decrease in your appetite or desires for food. And it doesn't always have to do with addictive foods, body types or where you are emotionally. Many women experience an increase in appetite just before their period starts. This is very common and doesn't mean that you're going to go over the top!

Sometimes we require different kinds and different amounts of food. For instance, I've noticed that when I ovulate, I tend to crave protein and my appetite increases. Because I follow my bodily cues, I eat more protein at this time (and, in fact, more in general). Years ago, I would have been thrown into a panic when my appetite increased, assuming that it meant I was about to go out of control because I didn't trust my body. Now I recognise that the increase in appetite is directly related to my natural body rhythm. Since I have ceased to eat out of emotional distress, I deduce that I must be hungry! But until I was aware of these connections, I used to worry about being extra hungry.

EATING TO MATCH YOUR BODY TYPE

Emotional or physical hunger?

I know that it can be hard to sort out the difference between a physical cue and an emotional impulse to eat. This is because we have overridden our bodies with our brains. Dieting is one way in which we do this. We let our heads dictate what we are going to do, regardless of what the body needs. This conditioning will take some sorting out. It is possible to regain that sense of communication with the body, but you must begin to trust it. Look at it this way. Your efforts to override your body have not given you the results you wanted, so why not try something new, like listening to your body!

Because we have such black-and-white thinking patterns and since we are so obsessed with our body weight, we want answers and we want them now! Preferably we want only one answer to the question of controlled eating. We want to grab hold of some solution and not let go. We want guarantees. But you have to start considering yourself as a changing and growing human being. Nothing in life is static. For example, adjustments in food are needed if: you have reduced or increased your physical output in a significant way; you are pregnant or lactating; you are ill; you change your environment (moving from a warm climate to a cool climate). These are just to name a few circumstances. And it is *natural* for everyone to make these adjustments.

Vitamins, minerals and stressful lives

Have you ever noticed a craving for certain foods when you have been feeling particularly stressed? When we are in a state of tension or stress, the B and C vitamins in our bodies are used up quite quickly. Since most of us feel that our lives are very stressful, it is worth noting the significance of vitamins and minerals in our lives. Some of our food cravings may be directly related to vitamin and mineral deficiencies. Again, your body is trying to talk to you so that you can rectify the situation and feel better.

Did you know, for example, that the B vitamins are responsible for converting food into energy, repairing body tissues, controlling fat metabolism and sustaining our nerves and muscles? They also act as an anti-depressant and have anti-allergic properties. The Bs are essential in the whole process of assimilation and digestion, and these are the ones we normally deplete first. It's no wonder people can have digestive difficulties when they're under stress. And if the digestive process isn't working properly, you're more likely to store food as fat than to utilise it as a source of energy. Vitamin C acts as an anti-oxidant. It increases the absorption of iron, controls cholesterol levels and helps maintain the body's resistance to infection.

We need to help our bodies maintain healthy vitamin levels by eating foods that contain them. Otherwise we operate at a lowered efficiency and our immune systems become vulnerable. It's much easier to get ill or catch some virus when our immune systems are weakened. Some good sources for your B vitamins are: yeast extract, liver, cheese, eggs, bran, nuts, chicken and wheat germ. Vitamin C is abundant in citrus fruits, leafy vegetables, tomatoes, parsley, kale and red peppers.

Remember that cooking does change the nutrient value of food. You should try to eat foods in as close to their natural state as possible. A good way of cooking food is the Chinese method of stir frying; This keeps food crisp, tasty and without having to use masses of oil or sauces.

Minerals are as fundamental as vitamins in the health of the body. They help with the circulation of blood and oxygen, assimilation of vitamins, growth, healing, proper organ functioning and reproduction. When someone is under stress or has experimented a lot with bizarre diets, there is the danger that they may be lacking in some of the essential minerals. Again, these deficiencies are often expressed by the body in cravings for certain types of foods. And the balance can be restored by knowing what foods contain which minerals. It's not necessary to take vitamin or mineral supplements unless you know that you have specific deficiencies or you really can't provide a balance of foods that can give you the vitamins you need.

I won't go into detail on all the vitamins and minerals – if you are interested, there are plenty of reference books on the topic. Besides, unless you actually know that you are deficient in certain areas, my feeling is that you are just taking a stab in the dark. I don't think there is any use in taking wild guesses at diagnosing for yourself. Get tested if you really want to know (see the Resources section). My point is that there are many reasons why you might be wanting to eat a certain food. We have to understand that there are real physical reasons for some of our eating, and it isn't just a matter of will-power or an underlying emotional issue that prompts our food desires.

How the mind influences the body

How do you know what your body needs? The physical, emotional and mental aspects of the body are interdependent. You have to start feeling that you and your body are one. Controlled eating is not just about eating 'healthy foods'. Negative thoughts also affect your health. How do you feel when you eat when you're angry, frustrated? How does it feel to eat when you are in a hurry? The body was designed to take in food as nourishment, not abuse. It's not designed to be overloaded. There may be things that you eat, or eat in particular ways, that actually inhibit proper absorption. You may be making your metabolism even less efficient without even knowing it. If you've dieted a lot, you probably already have a very confused body; your metabolism has probably slowed itself down. You need to help your body process your food in an efficient way. You don't want to become a warehouse for unassimilated food.

This adds pounds, and it can cause some nasty symptoms from accumulated waste pouring into your bloodstream.

Learning to listen to your body is the first step. We often ignore the signals for what we really need when we are obsessed. Work out what you really want. Is it food? If so, what kind of food do you want? Do you have any memory of how this type of food affects you?

Start taking your time. You're in no hurry. It's better to plan something that is actually going to satisfy you than to eat something quickly and be left wanting. That is one of the fundamental points that you need to remember. You are an individual and you need to have a way of eating that suits you! Otherwise you will set yourself up to fail, and you don't need any more of that. We will talk more about devising an individual plan in the final chapter.

HOMEWORK

PRACTICAL STEPS

- Take a look around your family. What type of body structures predominate? Can you identify what body type you might have? It might be helpful to look through photographs of yourself at different weights and see if your body shape has changed much. What kind of body type do you have? What do you expect your body to look like when it's at its natural weight? Is this realistic? Don't set yourself up to fail by thinking you can change your bodily structure. You can't argue with genetics!

- If you have difficulty knowing how you really look, do the exercise I described, making a cut-out of yourself.

- Experiment with eating to match your body type and see how you feel. (If this makes you feel in any way like you're dieting, then stop the experiment for the time being.)

WRITTEN EXERCISES

1 How do you feel about the body type that you have? Do you wish it were different?

2 Do you feel the characteristics I listed for your body type fit you?

3 If you want, you can keep a food diary for a week or so to compare the effects different foods seem to create for you. You don't have to put down quantity. We're not interested in how much, but rather *what kind* of food you eat and how it affects you.

4 Have you noticed any particular patterns in your appetite levels? What type of rhythmic cycle does your body go through in a month?

5 Have you noticed any correlation between your energy levels and eating?

155

11

PUTTING EXERCISE INTO PERSPECTIVE

B efore you decide to skip this chapter, let me say that you probably need less exercise than you think you should be having! And exercise coupled with dieting can lower your metabolism even more than just dieting alone. In fact, it can turn you into a slave of yet another obsession, which of course you don't need! This is why you need to know the facts about its benefits and drawbacks.

> *I had a client named Angela, who found herself in a vicious cycle. She had dieted over a number of years, restricting her intake more and more. The less she ate, the less she could eat and not gain weight. She had lowered her metabolism considerably. Because she still hadn't lost what she thought was enough weight, she decided to add exercise to her regime. By the time she came to me, she was exercising for five hours every day! And she didn't lose any more weight!*
>
> *Initially, the exercising helped her drop a few more pounds, but then it levelled out. She was certainly desperate because she felt she was doing absolutely everything she could do. Which, of course, she was. She just didn't know the facts about lowering metabolism, and now she found herself in position of stalemate. Surely, she thought, if she were to try to eat normally again, she would gain weight. And to make matters worse, she was not only obsessed with*

calorie counting, but with putting in her five hours a day at the gym!

She was depressed and at her wits' end. And quite under-standably so! She had done everything she thought she could possibly do to lose weight. And yet nothing was working, and she was very unhappy. Her relationship with her boyfriend was becoming quite tense because her attention was always on either dieting or exercising. He was getting fed up with her never having any time for him. She even stopped eating lunch so she could use that break from work to get in an extra hour on the trampoline she'd brought to the office! This was one unhappy lady. There was very little I could do for her, because she was determined to continue her regime.

Well-known television personality Oprah Winfrey is also in a similar position. Her most recent weight-loss scheme was to eat a low-fat diet and to exercise rigorously twice daily. She reported that she was up to running eight miles a day! She did manage to lose five stone, in approximately eight months, which is quite a feat. But now she is almost certainly in a position where she will have to maintain this type of eating and energy expenditure in order to retain her new size. It is possible, but will be very difficult to maintain over a long period of time. Some people who have gone on highly motivated exercise programmes (of which Oprah's certainly was one) can experience 'burnout', a loss of energy, purpose and sense of achievement produced by excessive exercise under stressful conditions.

I do have the utmost respect for Ms Winfrey, as she has shared her vulnerability about her weight obsession publicly over the years with millions of people. My feeling, though, is that her latest regime is a bit too arduous for the general population. Most people don't have the time or money to hire a personal cook and a trainer and then make time in their day to work out regularly in their own private studio.

My opinion is that people should start eating and exercising exactly as they intend to continue when their weight is where they want it. It's much better to incorporate an exercise plan that suits your capabilities and that fits your circumstances. That way you don't have to make any big adjustments one way or the other. And you won't gain weight back or have drastic changes in muscle tone if you don't follow your exercise routine to the letter. Many people give up exercise programmes because either they didn't lose any weight from it or it was too rigorous to follow in the long term. Unrealistic exercise schedules will become too difficult to maintain and they will be left by the wayside.

The dynamics of exercise

Most people that I come in contact with have a great deal of resistance to exercising regularly (myself included). Mine, as with many compulsives, is a love-hate relationship with exertion. I hate the idea of disciplining and motivating myself initially, but once I have started, I quite enjoy it. The usual reason for our resistance is thinking that you have to do a lot of exercise to make a difference. And for overweight people, the thought of moving an already heavy body through space seems too much of a task. It's very easy, with busy lives, to put it at the low end of the priority list. So what's the point of exercising at all?

Exercise helps people associate with their bodies and feel better about themselves. This can lead to improved body image and confidence. Exercise sends more oxygen throughout the body and stimulates the organs. It improves heart and lung functioning, tones muscles and makes you more flexible, which can make growing older more comfortable. It relieves tension, calms the nervous system and provides increased mental alertness. Exercise also releases endorphins (remember those great little chemicals in the brain that make you feel good?). Exercise doesn't sound so bad after all!

There are two kinds of exercise: **aerobic** and **anaerobic**. Their difference has to do with oxygen. Aerobic means 'with oxygen' and anaerobic mean 'without oxygen'. Aerobic exercise is any exercise that you can sustain for a period of twenty minutes or longer. It's the type of exercise that gets oxygen moving within your body and begins to burn off fat. Things like walking, swimming, cross-country skiing, stationary bicycling, skipping or jogging are considered aerobic. So, of course, is aerobic dance.

Anaerobic exercise doesn't burn fat. It's exercise that happens so quickly and is so intense that it can't be maintained. It pushes your lungs and heart to their limits. It's the type of activity that can only be done in short bursts, for example, tennis, body-building, football, volleyball. Anaerobic exercise is designed to develop strength, muscle tone and develop speed. Therefore, if you are looking to exercise for increasing your overall health, you should be looking more at aerobic exercise.

It's never too late to design a programme for yourself. But it is important, before embarking on any exercise regime, that you get yourself checked out by your doctor. You will need to know what your capabilities are so that you don't do yourself any damage. I know too many anorexics who feel compelled to exercise daily when they aren't even taking in enough nutrients to keep them standing up! And I know too many compulsive overeaters who want to take it all on at once. They end up over-exerting themselves and losing interest.

The most important thing about exercise is to do it because you know it will make you feel better physically and give you a better self-image. It should be simple, fun and well within your capabilities. Don't embark on anything that will make you feel more self-conscious. You want to build up a positive association with exercise.

The effect on weight

This may or may not be good news for you, depending on what type of answer you are looking for. Exercise doesn't make very much difference in terms of weight loss. Research has shown that exercise, unless done vigorously and on a calorie-reduced intake, will make very little difference to your weight. In an article in *Living*, January 1993, a US researcher, Stephen Pinney, reiterated the same findings. He followed changes in both the weight and metabolism of two groups of overweight women – one group dieting, another combining diet with exercise – over a period of several months. He found no significant differences in weight loss between the two groups, and when he examined changes in their respective metabolic rates, he understood why. While the diet-only group went down by ten per cent as their bodies strove to conserve fat, that of the diet-and-exercise group fell by a staggering twenty-seven per cent. In other words, the dual assault of restricting energy input while increasing output provoked a more extreme energy-conserving reaction.

This is shattering news for women who rely on exercise and dieting to keep their weight down. It suggests that they are simply digging themselves ever deeper into the SED (Subclinical Eating Disorder) trap while putting themselves at risk of weight gain in the long term.

Most exercise physiologists agree that you would need to do aerobic exercise for twenty or thirty minutes at least five times per week to make any difference at all to your weight. And even then it won't make much impact. It's not really the point of exercise. Exercise is for fitness not weight loss. If you feel guilty because you don't exercise enough, don't bother. It's not the one missing link to your weight, even though most of us don't exercise enough.

How much is enough?

There are so many videos, clubs and books to choose from, it's not always easy to know what to do or what to choose. The most important thing to consider is why you want to exercise and to establish your current physical abilities. Deciding what you are trying to accomplish with exercise will help determine how much you will want to do.

For basic general fitness, experts suggest that people do some type of aerobic exercise for twenty to thirty minutes three times per week. (Before you start visualizing yourself bulging out of some leotard, remember that walking is included in the aerobic exercise list!) If you're not up to doing aerobic exercise for whatever reason, there are simple stretching and 'soft' exercises that you could choose. I have listed some reference books on low-stress exercise in the Resources section.

Even if you only have ten or fifteen minutes a day to spend doing some simple stretches, you will be better off than not doing any exercise at all. If you don't have any time at all, then incorporate your exercise into your daily routine. Walk to places rather than drive. Get out in the garden and pull some weeds. Do some of that spring cleaning that you've been meaning to do. Instead of sitting in front of the television, get into a nice bath and do some stretching in there! It doesn't have to take a lot of your time and it doesn't have to feel bad!

Creating a personal exercise plan

Now that you know that exercise is not worth it as a means of losing weight, do you even want to exercise? Put exercise in perspective with your life. You probably don't have to do as much exercise as you think in order to benefit from it. For eating-disordered people, exercise can be a very good way of feeling like you are a part of your body. Usually we try to dissociate from it as much as we can. Don't feel that you have to buy any fancy machines or equipment, or become a member of a gym. There are many very good ways to tone up that don't cost anything. In fact, the trainer that Oprah paid to help her rated the number-one exercise in his opinion as walking!

HOMEWORK

PRACTICAL STEPS

- If you want to increase the amount of exercise you take, start by going to the library – they will have books that can guide you.

- Check your wardrobe for a comfortable outfit that you could use for exercise, and make sure that you have a pair of shoes which are easy to walk in and which don't rub or slip off.

- Take a look around your neighbourhood. Is there a place or route that would make a nice walk? (One that is safe and well lit if you intend going out after dark.)

- Find out if there are any leisure centres or swimming pools near you.

WRITTEN EXERCISES

1 Write down how much exercise you think you get in a week. Do you feel this is sufficient?

2 Make two lists: one of how you would benefit by starting or increasing your exercise and another of your reasons (or excuses) for not doing so. How do the two lists compare?

3 If you were to start or increase your exercise, what type of exercise would appeal to you? Is there any new type of exercise that you think you might like to try? If so, write down what type of clothing, equipment or facilities you would need in order to pursue this.

4 Write down ways in which you could get some more exercise within your normal daily routine. For example, 'I can walk to the shops instead of using my car', 'I can use the stairs at my office instead of the lift', etc.

5 Make some type of exercise one of your goals on your list from chapter 8. This needn't be ambitious. You can put, 'I walk for fun and fresh air for thirty minutes, three times a week'.

12

GETTING THROUGH SPECIAL OCCASIONS AND HOLIDAYS

W e all know the panic that arises when we receive an invitation to a social event. Immediately our hearts fall to our feet, we stop breathing and start wondering if we should accept the invitation or not. The dilemma begins. 'Oh, no, I feel fat, I don't want to go. And if I do go, what am I going to wear? Everything looks awful on me. The only decent clothes I have are now too tight!'

Then there is the matter of eating. 'Should I eat before I go, so I won't have to eat much there? Naturally, I'll want to partake in the goodies, but how can I be sure that I'll stop myself? Should I make a pact with myself about exactly how many drinks and how much food I'll have beforehand? Maybe I should just starve myself the day before and the day after, and then I don't have to worry about what I eat.'

Socialising can be a nightmare even before it begins. And it's not just because we of the body-hating, food dilemma club are paranoid. Sometimes people take the opportunity to address in public the very thing that we most fear: our body size and our food intake. It's bad enough if we have *our* attention on our bodies and food all the time, but when other people turn their attention on us, it feels like there really is no escape from this bodyism hell. But remember that what you eat and what size you are is nobody else's business!

> *Gayle told me that her husband gave her a difficult time every Christmas Day about what she ate. So she bought herself a T-shirt which she now wears every Christmas Day. It reads, 'I may be fat, but you're ugly and at least I can diet!'*

One of the things that really annoys me is going to a social event and listening to women discuss nothing but diets. It's particularly exasperating when the chatterers are thin and they know perfectly well that they have the best figures in the room. When people start talking incessantly about how they shouldn't be eating what they've just eaten, I want to start wringing necks! I couldn't care less about their paltry attempts to appease their own guilt. I just want to scream, 'Drop it and get a life!' I find it particularly boring that this is the highest level the conversation is going to reach. I'm tired of talking about the body. I don't care how many calories are in the paté. I just want to get on with things.

Christmas and holidays

Getting on with life is precisely the crux of my philosophy about Christmas and holidays. Foodwise, we need to put them into perspective. If you think of Christmas as 'This is the one day of the year when I must stuff myself because it is such a special day and I'm never going to get these goodies again', then you're setting yourself up for an anxious day and a distended stomach! However, if you think of Christmas as just another day, then it's not such a big deal. I'm not trying to diminish the specialness of holidays, I'm just trying to put food where it belongs. You don't have to eat it all in one day. Food is abundant. You can get what you want, whenever you want it. You can even make yourself some Christmas pudding in July, if you so wish!

MISTAKE NO. 1

One of the most common mistakes people make is to think that they need to shed a few pounds by dieting before Christmas. (Or before going on a holiday.) They think if they do that, they will be able to indulge during the holiday season and their weight will balance out. Wrong! Any time you radically restrict your intake, you slow down your metabolism. As soon as you start eating normally again, the weight will come back on and usually more quickly than what you think is reasonable. Besides, people don't eat normally during the holidays. They tend to eat more high-sugar, high-fat foods and more alcohol. They also tend to eat a lot more protein than their body can assimilate in any given sitting. This all adds up to many more calories than they generally consume. Outcome: weight gain.

Wouldn't you like to see just one January when you didn't think about embarking on another diet? No matter how many people tell you that they've found a revolutionary new diet that will take care of holiday weight gain, don't believe them. You can help yourself a great deal more if you try to eat as regularly as possible during the holidays. Don't try to diet! Your weight will remain more stable if you don't stuff yourself one day and starve yourself the next. Also, don't try to undertake any new, rigorous exercise plans during this time. It's unlikely that you'll be able to keep it up because there is so much going on, and you'll only feel disappointed with yourself. Instead, it would be better if you just got out into the fresh air for a fifteen- to twenty-minute walk to help rebalance yourself.

Practise sensible food choices

Allow yourself treats, but try to keep your consumption of sugar and alcohol to a minimum. Keep your eye on the addictive foods that we talked about in chapter 9 and you will save yourself many empty calories and not distort your appetite. High-fat foods (rich, creamy foods) can add a lot of calories. And remember, these types of food usually go down so quickly that your stomach doesn't have time to register that you've had plenty of calories until you've eaten so much that you feel overly full.

MISTAKE NO. 2

Do your best to maintain a balance, not feeling too full or too empty. Feeling out of balance generally precipitates more impulsive eating behaviour. If you are too hungry and are feeling deprived, you are more likely to overeat to compensate. If you are too full, you may feel you have already blown it, so you might as well go all the way. And certainly this state of being too full will almost certainly make you feel worse about yourself. Remember, compulsive overeating isn't a sign of inadequacy. It isn't a crime. And you shouldn't be punished for it. Most people over-indulge during Christmas! You're not a freak!

But if you do find you've over-indulged, give your digestion a break. Don't continue to overload it the next day with foods that are difficult to process. Drink fruit juices or eat fresh fruit. That is the easiest food for your body to handle. Eat simpler meals for a day. Try to ease the strain on your body. If you don't continue to feel bloated, then you are more likely to be able to take your attention off your body and stop feeling guilty.

Be realistic

Holidays are difficult times, full of emotion for everyone. Be compassionate with yourself. If you have to put up with relatives that drive you round the bend, you need to be nice to yourself! You only have to get through one day at a time. You don't have to organise the entire season in one go. Keep in contact with your support network, wherever they may be. You may need to talk yourself through some feelings (whether high or low). You need to feel that you have support, no matter what time of the year it is. You don't have to be alone with your feelings. And if no one is available, write down how you feel. This will help to release energy so you won't feel compelled to eat out of repressed feelings.

Don't torture yourself

MISTAKE NO. 3

Don't keep stockpiles of food around that are going to worry you. Do your shopping daily if need be and buy only the things you need immediately. If you have leftovers that you think will bother you the next day, throw them out. If you think you are likely to rummage in the bin later on to retrieve them (and some of us have been known to do this!), squirt washing-up liquid over your leftovers so they're no longer tempting. Believe me, I've soaped a fair bit of food in my day. It was actually a very helpful thing to do. Then I was free of the leftovers and not thinking about them the rest of the day. This is not wasting food or money. This is helping yourself when you need a little extra assistance. Think of how often you have spent money on binges – that *is* wasting money!

If you are the host . . .

If you are hosting a dinner or party, make it as easy on yourself as you can. You can even purchase some ready-made foods from a delicatessen or restaurant so you don't have to go to the trouble of cooking. If you do cook, make as many things in advance as you can. That way, if you want to test your dishes, you can do so enough in advance so you won't get too full.

MISTAKE NO. 4

Make sure you're not already full when your party starts because you tested everything while making it. Make your tasting a meal instead of unconscious picking. Put it on a plate, sit down and eat it. This will stop you nibbling. Be sure to have food available for yourself that you can eat without feeling guilty. If you're not drinking alcohol, provide a tasty alternative for yourself. You can make a glass of orange juice or tomato juice look like a mixed drink. There is also some very tasty low-alcohol beer and wine on the market and some sparkling fruit juices. Since the party is in your home, you have much more control over what is provided.

MISTAKE NO. 5

Don't feel that you have to provide massive quantities of superior food for everyone in order for them to enjoy their evening. Since there are so many social events over the holidays, people might enjoy attending at least one dinner party where they *don't* feel obliged to eat a lot of rich foods.

If you are dining out

The first thing to remember is that socialising is about enjoying the company of others. Focus your attention on the people you are with and not the food. Don't be lured into mistake no. 2 again, which is starving yourself before you go out. Eat as you would on any day. You are less likely to want to overeat or to go out of balance emotionally if you keep your day as ordinary as possible.

If you are at a buffet, put a variety of food on your plate and then eat half of everything that you took. This way you won't feel that you had to sacrifice tasting different items, and it will prevent you from getting too full.

MISTAKE NO. 6

Don't make hasty decisions. Eat slowly to give yourself time to think and make the best choice. If you find yourself with too much food on your plate, you can push the food around a bit, taking small bites so it looks as though you're eating all of it when you're not. You can engage in conversation. When people are eating, they're not generally paying attention to what anyone but themselves is eating. You can pass a lot of time by talking to others while they eat, and then you don't have to finish what's on your plate. (Unless, of course, you want to!)

If you are feeling anxious, buy yourself some time. Excuse yourself to the toilet. Go and be by yourself for a few minutes to talk yourself through what you want to do next. Get into the habit of going over your mental checklist when you start to feel anxious or confused about food. Ask yourself, 'Am I really hungry? What do I want to get out of this evening? How can I make this as easy on myself as possible?'

MISTAKE NO. 7

Never refuse food by announcing that you're watching your weight or calories. It doesn't put people off if they're trying to get you to eat. People are often afraid they will offend their host by not eating everything that is offered. If a simple 'No, thank you' isn't enough for them, acknowledge the host's efforts: 'I can see that you put a lot of energy into this, and it looks lovely, but I just couldn't eat another bite.' People are often looking for recognition that what they served was tasty and that you enjoyed it. So make sure that message gets across: 'I had a bite and it was delicious.'

Take care of yourself

If you're worried about what's being served, ring your host up in advance and ask about the menu. If you're worried about what's on offer, make sure that you take along a few things you need, for example your own juice or salad or something that you like. On the one hand, you don't want to feel different from the others – you certainly don't want to feel deprived – but you also need to make sure that there is food or drink available that won't make you anxious. It's no good socialising if your mind is going to be on food all night!

Before any event

Prepare yourself for special occasions and holidays. Sit down and make a list of your priorities.

- What is your aim with this holiday or special day?
- What do you want to get out of it?
- Are your expectations realistic?
- Do you need to alter them?
- How are you going to make it as easy on yourself as you can?
- What foods or circumstances do you need to provide for yourself?

For any function or holiday, be sure to have clothing that makes you feel good about yourself. There is nothing worse than being stuck in an outfit that only draws attention to your body in a negative way, either because you think you look hideous in it or because it's uncomfortable. You'll enjoy any occasion a great deal more if you are physically comfortable.

Easy treat substitutes

It amazes me how many people have never visited a health-food shop or even know about other food choices. There are so many things that are tasty without being addictive or full of chemicals. Using these foods is another way that you can help yourself, particularly through periods when everyone around you is stuffing themselves with high-calorie, low-nutrition foods. Do take the time to do some exploring for yourself. As I mentioned earlier, there are some nice carob bars that make a great substitute for chocolate if you want to avoid that. Just make sure that they are not sweetened with sugar. Not all 'health' foods are as natural as they claim!

There are also many ways that you can sweeten food without having to use sugar or artificial sweeteners. (Artificial sweeteners are as good as useless; you are simply putting chemicals in your body.) Some good sweeteners are: brown rice syrup, barley malt syrup and fruit juice concentrate. You can use these instead of sugar or honey, and they can be found at health-food shops.

There are wonderful sugar-free fruit spreads that you can substitute for sugar-filled jams. And there is a terrific snack called halva (it comes from the Middle East) which is a sesame-seed sweetmeat sweetened with either grape juice or honey. Buy the one with grape juice.

And don't forget that wonderful snack food, popcorn. This makes a great treat because it's loaded with fibre and you can eat mounds of it without eating many calories. (Unless of course, you smother it with butter or syrup!)

These are just a few suggestions, things that I use. Be creative – satisfy yourself. Explore what other foods are out there that you don't even know about. Eating well doesn't have to be boring, nor do you have to feel deprived. And of course, you need to allow yourself to eat exactly what you want!

HOMEWORK

PRACTICAL STEPS

- Remind yourself that it's very common for *everyone* to indulge themselves on special occasions and holidays. This isn't something that only compulsive eaters do! Try to sort out for yourself how many of your food desires at these times are linked with actually being hungry, as opposed to 'mouth hunger' or social pressure.

- Make yourself a chart of how many special occasions or holidays you think you will be participating in over the next month. (Do this month by month.) Make a note as to whether or not you will be providing or cooking food for any of these events. Put an asterisk next to any circumstance you feel shaky about. (We will deal with this in written exercise 2.)

- Don't volunteer to provide or cook food for any event

that you feel will be an ordeal for you. This is very important!

- Try not to avoid socialising because of the fear of overeating. Instead, practise the suggestion of focusing your attention on the people and your interactions with them.

WRITTEN EXERCISES

1 Write down how you feel about holidays and special occasions in general. What is important to you about them? What is uncomfortable about them? What links do these feelings have with your childhood experiences?

2 Take your chart of expected occasions and look at the ones you have marked. Write down what you feel will be difficult about those particular occasions and why. Make a plan for how you intend to get yourself through each event.

3 Make a list of all the foods

that you associate with birthdays, parties, holidays, etc. Do you feel you can enjoy these foods too? If not, why?

4 Now make a list of specific foods that you are going to allow yourself to have on the occasions that you are planning to attend.

13

SUCCESS AS A LIFELONG PROCESS

🐾 *'Diet is not the key to anything sublime. Diet is just food. It is vital, physical activity. You cannot become absolutely healthy simply by manipulating the diet, because diet only deals with the body.* 🐾

[From 'Diet Is Not the Key to Salvation', in *The Eating Gorilla Comes in Peace* by Adi Da copyright (Avatara Dau Loloma Pty, Ltd., as trustee for the Avatara Dau Loloma Sacred Trust). Used with permission.]

What worked for me was to take everything into account, on an emotional, physical, behavioural and spiritual level. I needed to look at everything, and when that was done, I needed to relax and just get on with my life. When I did this, I noticed how much more there was in life besides worrying about food and eating. I began to develop relationships that were deeper and more intimate than I had ever done before. I also realised that *I* was the one obsessed with my weight!

When you're self-conscious, it's easy to feel paranoid, convinced that everyone is watching what you eat or what you weigh. But I discovered that people don't really have the time or interest to care. They're all too busy with their own lives. Ultimately, no one cares what size I am. I'm the one who's over-concerned. I know this seems completely obvious to many, but to those of us obsessed with weight or food, this is new information! It's amazing, when your attention isn't always on yourself, how much else there is in life to see and do. As I started to turn my attention to other people and things, my extra weight continued to peel off.

I didn't count calories. And I certainly would never even dream of dieting again, because I didn't have to in order to recover from compulsive eating. Nor do you. You can learn to live without being encumbered with self-loathing for your body. You don't have to be fat, nor do you have to take drugs or starve yourself. In my process of recovery, there were a number of things that helped me a great deal and a number of things that just made life more difficult.

What helped

- Attending a self-help group. I learned that I wasn't alone in my suffering and that there were many people who understood the problems I faced.
- Learning to express myself and taking assertiveness training. I discovered there was a big difference between being aggressive and being assertive, and it had a direct relationship to getting what I wanted.
- Finding out I wasn't crazy, I was only compulsive.
- Giving up sugar altogether until I could get some objective distance from it. This decreased my bingeing by about ninety per cent.
- Learning more about the interactions between food, the body and emotions.
- Learning other ways to nurture myself that weren't food related.
- Learning how to feel good in my body by doing things that felt good, for example swimming, having a massage, having a facial.

What didn't help

- Going to doctors, therapists and other professionals who didn't know anything about eating disorders or weight.
- Dieting, vomiting, diet pills, laxatives. These all exacerbated the problem.
- Having a secret life, hiding myself away.
- 'Contemplating my navel' – focusing most of my time on my weight or food.
- Constantly weighing myself.
- Being hard on myself.

Make the effort to succeed

There is no reason why you shouldn't be able to recover from compulsive eating naturally. And I don't mean this in a flippant way. But it will take some time and a lot of energy on your part. You're going to need to be very patient with yourself. You have a lot to do. You have years of reinforcing negative attitudes and self-destructive behaviour to get rid of. You have belief systems that set you up to fail. I'm not talking about just trying to convince yourself that things are positive or that you like yourself or your body, even though it's not really what you feel. You need to get in touch with *why* you think and feel the way that you do. But you don't have to wait until you can answer your questions to progress. You need to pin-point exactly what your particular dilemmas are. There must be a clash of feelings somewhere in you or you would be relaxed about eating and your body. It may be that your conflict is that you want to overeat and be thin at the same time. Or you may be fearful of being successful. You may be afraid that you'd change too much and would become a different person if you really allowed yourself to be the person you want to be.

176

As I keep saying, your problem is not your weight. Your problem is that you are unhappy with yourself. You need to explore what is keeping you unhappy and frustrated and to release your negative associations with your body. You need to begin identifying yourself with your body and to demystify food and put it into perspective. And you need to begin using alternative methods of coping that can get you moving in a positive direction so you don't have to remain in this self-destructive cycle. You're not bad or inadequate because of how you look or who you are. You're a human being just like the rest of us. We all have our finer points and our rough edges. We all make mistakes. We are all looking for the same thing; to be loved and to love.

Hating your body is very self-destructive. This attitude isn't going to help you recover from compulsive eating. I was speaking to a woman who told me that she thought her weight problem was purely physical. She said that she didn't have any emotional problems about it. I asked her if she liked her body. She said, 'No, I hate my body.' So I said, 'It sure sounds to me like you have an emotional problem!' Become compassionate with yourself. Lower your expectations. They are too high. Relax with who you are. Trust your body and let it become your friend. It will help you. Stop working against it. You don't have to *prove* that you are lovable.

STEPS TO SUCCESS
- Continue exploration and expression
- Relax attention
- Experiment with food – designer eating
- Re-associate with your body
- Change attitude and tastes
- Build self-esteem
- Experiment with responsible eating and make behavioural changes
- Begin self-exploration and break the deprivation mentality
- Accept the situation – reality stance
- Stop dieting – take stock

Compulsive eating is never purely a physical matter because we are not just flesh and bones. You must think of yourself as body, mind and spirit all together. You do not live in a vacuum. We think, feel, take in nourishment and participate in relationships. So it only makes sense that you need to look at all these areas for answers. The body and mind work together. Express yourself. Allow yourself to explore. Have a massage, get some aromatherapy. Look into alternative forms of exercise. Learn to **meditate**. There are lots of complementary practices that could help you. Take good care of yourself.

DON'T WASTE YOUR TIME

It seems almost ludicrous that the majority of my life energy has been taken up by trying to lose weight. You don't have to waste precious years doing the same thing. Remember that you're in the middle of a process, and the process is called life. There's no prize at the end. Being a size 10 doesn't mean that you've won! Being overweight or being a compulsive eater can be a symptom that you are unhappy, or at least that there is a conflict going on between you and your body. It doesn't mean that you're stupid or inadequate. Some days you'll do better than others. You will go through phases. Don't let your impatience and low self-esteem guide you.

You must also remember that everyone ages and dies. So if you are pinning all your hopes of happiness on what your body looks like, you're only going to be disappointed. Everybody gets wrinkles! The body changes with age. You can slow the ageing process down by taking good care of yourself, but you can't stop it. Live in the present. So many of my clients have already decided that they are not going to be happy until their weight changes, or until they feel they have completely recovered.

Some helpful reminders

- Go over your mental checklist **before** you eat.
  Am I hungry?
  How am I feeling?
  What do I want?
  Is food what I want?
  What kinds of food do I want?
  Will it make me feel better about myself?
- Buy clothes that fit you now! Don't wear tight clothing.
- Develop a support system for yourself.
- Get counselling for issues that you need to discuss in depth.
- Make affirmations every day. Develop a positive mental attitude.

I hope this has been helpful for you. There is really nothing else that you need to know. All the answers are within yourself. Be gentle with yourself. Let your heart guide you. That is the definitive answer!

HOMEWORK

PRACTICAL STEPS

- Go back through this book and do any of the exercises that you missed the first time through.
- Use the book as a point of reference whenever you feel lost. Reread sections as you need them – you'll often get new understandings and perspectives, as sometimes we miss things the first time and it takes another round to fully absorb what is helpful.

WRITTEN EXERCISES

Instead of the usual question section, I've provided a checklist for you to use, initially on a daily basis. After a period of time (you will know instinctively when), change it to a weekly exercise. This isn't used for reproaching yourself for falling short – it's a tool for noticing how well you are doing and also to help you focus your attention and pick up on any areas that need more nurturing. Make use of it until the different elements become second nature to you. (You may want to make a photocopy of it while it's still blank so that you can have it for a number of months.) Just tick off what you feel you've been able to do.

THIS WEEK I . . .

	M	TU	W	TH	F	SA	SU
Ate without guilt.							
Noticed how I was feeling before I ate.							
Ate slowly and breathed throughout.							
Treated my body with tenderness.							
Went over my goals.							
Had a special treat (food or otherwise).							
Took some time for myself.							
Asked for help when I needed it.							
Expressed how I was feeling.							
Allowed someone to nurture me.							
Put energy into my appearance.							
Took some exercise.							

14

YOUR
QUESTIONS
ANSWERED

O ver the course of my teaching and counselling work, I get asked a lot of questions pertaining to recovery and success. Many of these questions are exactly the same, no matter where I am or who I'm with. I have included some of the most frequently asked questions, so you can have the answers for yourself.

CAN I RECOVER COMPLETELY FROM COMPULSIVE EATING?

Yes, absolutely! You don't have to live your life obsessed with food or your body. It's possible to recover completely from anorexia, bulimia or compulsive eating. But recovery does takes time, patience and determination. You do have to be willing to give your recovery at least as much time and attention as you have put into dieting or compulsive eating.

Recovery to me means:

- freedom from being obsessed about food or the body;
- feeling that eating is simply an ordinary act of maintaining health and well-being;
- eating without guilt or reprisal from oneself;
- the absence of binge eating or out-of-control eating.

I and the many women whom I've counselled or who have taken my seminars have made major changes in our lives and our relationship to food. My life is not ruled by food or any obsession to be thinner than what is healthy. Bingeing ceased for me many years ago. I have no preoccupation with calories or guilt about eating. I think of food as something positive, that nourishes my body and helps me to feel well. I enjoy everything I eat, and I love to eat food that tastes great. I choose what I eat intuitively. I let my body do the deciding as to what it wants and needs. I eat to feel good in my body and to have energy. And I'm not deprived of anything that I might want. Recovery for me also includes feeling free to be and look like me.

HOW LONG DOES RECOVERY TAKE?

There is no way I can give you a time scale for how long it will take, because it's different for everyone. Each person's circumstances and worries will play a part in their recovery process. You can only proceed as quickly as you're able or comfortable. You can't rush recovery; you need to be emotionally ready to take each step. Recovery is a process, and there will be varying degrees of progress at each level. You will know, however, when you've recovered, because you will notice that you are not preoccupied with food or your weight or eating! You will know that you've recovered when you can leave one chip on your plate because you are full up! You will know that you've recovered when your weight or what you have eaten for the day has no bearing on making decisions about your social life!

IF I EAT WHAT I WANT, WON'T I GO OUT OF CONTROL AND GAIN WEIGHT?

This is the biggest question that I get asked. And it's the hardest thing that I have to convince people of. Going out of control is unlikely if you are eating when you are truly hungry. What generally happens is when people begin to relax about what they allow themselves to eat, their reasons for overeating diminish. If you really let yourself eat what you want, you begin to lose the desire or the need to eat it secretly, or to eat as much as you can get your hands on. It's the deprivation mentality that produces overeating and bingeing. Sometimes people may eat a bit more at first when they experiment with eating what they want, but this usually subsides in a short period of time. Fear is what keeps people stuck feeling that they can't trust their bodies to tell them what to eat. It's not your body that has gone out of control, it's your mind! Instead of worrying about your body betraying you, you should concentrate on what you programme your mind to believe.

WHAT IF I DON'T WANT TO GIVE UP SUGAR OR CHOCOLATE?

You don't have to do anything you don't want to do, or anything that you don't feel ready to do. Remember that the first premise of this recovery programme is that you must get over your deprivation mentality. Once you actually believe that you can eat whatever you want, whenever you want, then you may be ready to move on to more experimentation with foods. The only problem with sugar and chocolate is that they are addictive substances and they may be sabotaging your efforts. So, instead of trying to give them up completely, you may want to make choices about when, where and how much you have around. My suggestion is that if they are torture foods for you, then don't keep them in your house.

SHOULDN'T I EAT THREE MEALS A DAY?

Don't eat if you're not hungry! If you are hungry for three meals a day, then eat them. But there's no sense in eating by the clock. You must adapt yourself to an eating plan that fits your appetite, needs and circumstances. There are many theories about eating (what to eat, when and how much) but they are all useless if you don't feel that they are beneficial to you. Experimentation is how you'll find out what suits you. Be flexible. Sometimes you'll feel like eating more or less than other times, depending on bodily needs and energy expenditure.

WILL MY BODY REALLY GO BACK INTO BALANCE?

Everyone's body has a natural 'set point' or weight that it likes to maintain. This is a natural occurrence. If you let your body choose how much and what type of foods to eat, your body will find its natural set point. Your set point may not be quite as low as you might like, but you won't have to struggle to keep it there unless you begin dieting or throwing your body out of balance with starving and bingeing. Your body wants to be in balance. This is another area where you will need faith and patience. Depending on how long you have been confusing your metabolism, it may take a while for your body to settle back into its natural state.

WHAT IF I RELAPSE?

Count on it! Don't be surprised if this happens. You're not perfect. You're learning to cope in a whole new way. I actually prefer to call it 'phasing' because I think it's a more accurate description. This is life. This isn't a diet that you either do well with or not. Everyone is bound to have days or weeks where they do better. It doesn't mean that you are still not recovering. It just means that you're in a difficult phase of recovery. Sometimes I would binge and think, 'Why did I do that again?' I think it was a good reminder to me *why* I was trying to change my methods of coping.

You are bound to have some difficulties because you have been repressing feelings with food, and those feelings are going to have the freedom to surface. Distress is an opportunity for continued growth.

SHOULD I TELL MY FAMILY AND FRIENDS THAT I AM TRYING TO RECOVER FROM COMPULSIVE EATING?

Yes. This is a very good way to get some support for yourself. Don't worry about being embarrassed. You haven't got some disgusting abnormality, you've simply developed the habit of using food as a coping strategy. You're not crazy. You're compulsive. Choose those closest to you to share your hopes and fears. Let them help you where they can.

HOW CAN A FAMILY MEMBER OR FRIEND HELP ME?

They can help in a number of ways. They don't have to understand compulsive eating altogether in order to support you. Most people who haven't suffered an eating disorder find it very difficult to understand why a person turns to food in the way we do, so don't feel you have to get them to understand before they can help (though they can be a greater source of support for you if they have educated themselves a bit about compulsive eating).

The most important thing they can do is be available to listen to you. You've spent too much time bottling up your feelings and you need to have some outlet for expressing them.

They can help by not making any reference to what you are or aren't eating. You can let them know what concepts of recovery you are working with and then they should let you get on with it. This is particularly helpful if you feel you need to eat ice-cream as a steady diet for a few days. If you let them know the philosophy of this programme, then they won't think you have gone off the rails!

THERE SEEM TO BE SOME PARADOXES IN YOUR APPROACH TO RECOVERY. ON ONE HAND, YOU SUGGEST EATING WHATEVER YOU WANT, AND ON THE OTHER HAND YOU TALK ABOUT FOOD COMBINING.

Yes. Just as in life, there are paradoxes. It won't seem so ambiguous if you can see that this process of recovery is in stages. Before you could ever even consider giving up a certain food or experimenting with it, you must first pass through the level of feeling that you can eat whatever you like. Once this is in place, then you can move on to investigate other foods and how they make you feel. If you allow yourself to take the time that you need for each level of recovery, then you will know instinctively when to move on to next level. Don't be afraid to trust your body or your heart to tell you what to do next.

186

SHOULD I GO TO A COUNSELLOR?

I would highly recommend seeing a trained counsellor (preferably someone with an understanding of eating disorders) under any of the following conditions:

- If you feel lonely and have no support system for yourself.
- If you feel there is no one who will understand your concerns.
- If eating, food or your weight is preoccupying your time and attention.
- If you are obsessed with being slim.
- If you feel that your eating behaviour is out of control.
- If your friends or family are concerned about your weight or your eating behaviour.
- If you hate your body.
- If you suspect that you may have an eating disorder.
- If you are on a merry-go-round of dieting.

WHAT IS THE SINGLE MOST IMPORTANT THING THAT BECAME A TURNING POINT FOR YOU IN YOUR RECOVERY?

There is actually a fairly simple answer to that. Even though I had spent time discovering and expressing my feelings and uncovering the things that motivated me in life, there was a major turning point that put me on the road to freedom.

This occurred when I was thirty-three years old. Having just reached fourteen and a half stone *without* overeating and having gone on a fast for six weeks without losing weight, I finally gave up dieting forever. I decided that I would never ever diet again, and I began to accept my body for the size that it was. I didn't like how it looked, but I accepted that that was the size I was and I would not spend another moment worrying about it. I knew that I had to take my attention off my body as a sign of my worth and put it on higher things. And if I only had one sentence in which to tell you how to recover from compulsive eating, I would have to say: take your eyes off your thighs and stop making yourself a problem that needs fixing!

REFERENCES

Adi Da, *The Eating Gorilla Comes in Peace*, Middletown, California, The Dawn Horse Press, 1979

Adi Da, *Conscious Exercise and the Transcendental Sun*, Middletown California, The Dawn Horse Press, 1984

Airola, Paavo, *Are You Confused?*, Phoenix, Arizona, Health Plus Publishers, 1977

American Psychiatric Association, *Diagnostic and Statistical Manual (DSM III) of Mental Disorders*, third edition (revised), Washington DC, 1987

Atkinson, Louise, 'Farewell to the Hourglass Figure' in the *Daily Mail*, 16 February 1994

Bailey, Covert, *Fit or Fat*, Boston, Houghton-Mifflin, 1978

Balaskas, Arthur and Stirk, John, *Soft Exercise: The Complete Book of Stretching*, London, Unwin Paperbacks, 1983

Bennett, W. and Gurin, J., *The Dieter's Dilemma*, New York, Basic Books, 1982

Bircher, Ruth, *Eating Your Way to Health*, London, Faber, 1966

Boakes, Robert, Popplewell, David and Burton, Michael (eds), *Eating Habits, Food, Physiology and Learned Behaviour*, Chicester, John Wiley and Sons, 1987

Bovey, Shelley, *Being Fat Is Not a Sin*, London, Pandora, 1989

Bray, George, 'Obesity in America: An Overview of the Second Fogarty International Centre Conference on Obesity', Washington, *The International Journal of Obesity*, 1979

Brown, Millie, *Low-Stress Fitness: An Easy-Does-It Exercise Plan For Any Age, Stretching, Walking, Bicycling and Swimming*, Tucson, Arizona, The Body Press, 1985

Bruch, Hilde, *Eating Disorders: Obesity, Anorexia Nervosa and the Person Within*, New York, Basic Books, 1973

Buckroyd, Julia, *Eating Your Heart Out*, London, Optima, 1989

Cannon, G. and Einzig, H., *Dieting Makes You Fat*, London, Century, 1973

Chernin, Kim, *The Obsession: Reflections on the Tyranny of Slenderness*, New York, Harper and Row, 1981

Crisp, A. H., *Anorexia Nervosa: Let Me Be*, London, Academic Press, 1980

Dowling, Colette, *The Cinderella Complex*, London, Fontana, 1982

Duffy, William, *Sugar Blues*, Radnor, Pennsylvania, Chilton, 1975

Eating Disorders Association Annual General Report, *Dying to Be Slim*, Norwich, 1993

Fairburn, Christopher G. and Wilson, G. Terence (eds), *Binge Eating, Nature, Assessment and Treatment*, London, The Guilford Press, 1993

Gardiner, Rebecca, 'Diet Addiction' in *Options*, January 1993

Garner, David M. and Garfinkel, Paul E., *Handbook of Psychotherapy for Anorexia and Bulimia*, London, The Guilford Press, 1985

Grant, Doris and Joice, Jean, *Food Combining for Health*, London, Thorsons, 1984

Greenhalgh, Dr T., 'Why Fat Is a Wobbly Issue', London, *The Times*, 28 July 1994

Greenhalgh, Dr T., 'Running on Empty', *The Times*, London, 14 August 1994

Hall, Nicola, *The Treatment of Disorderly Eating: Anorexia and Bulimia – Drugs or Psychotherapy?*, Eating Disorders Association Essay Competition, Aston University, Birmingham, 1992

Haskew, Paul and Adams, Cynthia H., *When Food Is a Four-Letter Word*, New Jersey, Prentice-Hall, 1984

Kano, Susan, *Never Diet Again*, London, Thorsons, 1990

Lawrence, Marilyn and Dana, Mira, *Fighting Food – Coping with Eating Disorders*, London, Penguin Books, 1990

Lewith, George, Kenyon, Julian and Dowson, David, *Allergy and Intolerance – A Complete Guide to Environmental Medicine*, London, Green Print, 1992

Living, March 1988, 'Are You A Chocaholic?'

Living, January 1993, 'Are You a Victim of Compulsive Eating?'

Logue, A. W., *The Psychology of Eating and Drinking*, New York, W. H. Freeman and Company, 1986

Mayer, J., *Overweight – Causes, Cost and Control*, New Jersey, Prentice-Hall, 1969

Metropolitan Life Insurance Company, *Metropolitan Height and Weight Tables*, New York, 1983

Nakken, Craig, *The Addictive Personality*, New York, Hazeldon, 1988

Nelson, Dennis, *Food Combining Simplified*, Santa Cruz, D. Nelson, 1988

Nelson, Dennis, *Maximizing Your Nutrition*, Santa Cruz, D. Nelson, 1988

Orbach, Susie, *Fat Is a Feminist Issue*, New York, Paddington Press, 1978

Orminski, Linda, *You Count, Calories Don't*

Patano, Patricia and Savage, Linette, *Muscle Aerobics, The Ultimate Workout for Body Shaping*, Tucson, Arizona, The Body Press, 1985

Robbins, Anthony, *Awaken the Giant Within*, London, Simon and Schuster, 1992

Roth, Geneen, *Breaking Free from Compulsive Eating*, London, Plume, 1993

Royal College of Psychiatrists, *Eating Disorders Fact Sheet*, London, 1991

Saunders, Kate, 'Absolutely Plumptious' in *She*, May 1994

Shelton, Herbert, *Food Combining Made Easy*, Tampal, Natural Hygiene Press, 1968

Stuart, R. B. and Davis, B., *Slim Chance in a Fat World – Behavioral Control of Obesity*, Champaign, Illinois, Research Press, 1972

Stunkard, A., *The Pain of Obesity*, Palo Alto, Bell Publishing, 1976

Trowbridge, John Parks and Walker, Morton, *The Yeast Syndrome*, London, Bantam, 1986

West, Richard, *Eating Disorders: Anorexia Nervosa and Bulimia Nervosa*, Office of Health Economics, London, 1994

Yudkin, John, *Pure, White and Deadly*, Harmondsworth, Penguin.

RESOURCES

HELPFUL PEOPLE

The Author

You may contact me for individual counselling or intensive weekend courses. I do take my course around the country and am also available for public speaking.

Genevieve Blais, MSW
Offices at: Harley Street, London W1
              The Woburn Centre, Norwich
Correspondence to: Tasburgh Hall, Lower Tasburgh, Norwich, Norfolk, NR15 1NA

The Centre for the Study of Complementary Medicine

They offer help for Candida, ME (myalgic encephalomyelitis – chronic fatigue), allergies and environmental sensitivities. They can test you for food sensitivities and intolerances. A word of warning: they are expensive. These are the people who wrote the book *Allergy and Intolerance.*

Offices at: 51 Bedford Place
              Southampton
              Hampshire SO1 2DG   Phone: 01703-334752

              14 Harley House
              Upper Harley Street
              London NW1 4PR   Phone: 0171-9357848

Complementary Medicine Services

They have people who travel around the country giving the vega test. They are very reasonable and can tell if you have any food sensitivities as well as vitamin and mineral deficiencies.

Office at: 9 Corporation Street
                 Taunton, Somerset   Phone: 01823–325022

The Eating Disorders Association

They are primarily a resource for anorexics and bulimics. However, they can give information on private counsellors working with eating disorders throughout Great Britain. They can also refer you to self-help groups around the country designed for anorexics, bulimics and compulsive eaters, and they have some very useful literature.

Sackville Place
44 Magdalen Street
Norwich
Norfolk NR3 1JU
Telephone help line: 01603–621414   Mon.–Fri. 9 a.m.–6.30 p.m.
For the under-eighteens, ring: 01603–765050   Mon., Tues., Wed. 4 p.m.–6.30 p.m.

Overeaters Anonymous

This is the self-help group with the same set-up as Alcoholics Anonymous.

140a Tachbrook Street
London SW1   Phone: 0171–498 5505
Their literature is available from:

Quest Books
River House
46 Lea Road
Waltham Abbey
Essex EN9 1AT

HELPFUL PUBLICATIONS

There are a lot of books that I have read over the years that have helped me. I have chosen just a few, so as not to bombard you with information.

Allergy and Intolerance – A Complete Guide to Environmental Medicine by George Lewith, Julian Kenyon and David Dowson, Green Print, London, 1992

It's not as heavy as it sounds! This is the book that explained all my vague symptoms.

Conscious Exercise and the Transcendental Sun by Adi Da, The Dawn Horse Press, 1984

This can be ordered through Free Daist Books, Lower Tasburgh, Norwich, Norfolk NR15 1NA, phone: 01508-470574. A whole-body concept of exercise through calisthenics, gentle stretching and Hatha Yoga for standing, sitting, walking and breathing properly.

The Eating Gorilla Comes in Peace by Adi Da, The Dawn Horse Press, 1979

This can be ordered through Free Daist Books, Lower Tasburgh, Norwich, Norfolk NR15 1NA, phone: 01508-470574. This is one of the most comprehensive books you will ever find on diet and health. It addresses the relationship between body, mind and spirit.

Food Combining for Health by Doris Grant and Jean Joice, Thorsons Publishers, London, 1984

An uncomplicated book that can help you understand food combining and how to do it.

Sugar Blues by William Duffy, Chilton, Radnor, Pennysylvania, 1975

Explains the history and facts about sugar and what it does in the body. Easy to read. After reading this book, I was able to break my sugar addiction.

Fat Is a Feminist Issue by Susie Orbach,
Hamlyn, London, 1982

This has become one of the classics for compulsive eaters, though she does go a bit over the top in relating everything to feminism.

Eating Your Heart Out by Julia Buckroyd,
Optima, London, 1989

This consists largely of case examples that point out the emotional aspects involved in overeating. Written by a British therapist.

Pure, White and Deadly by John Yudkin

This is the British equivalent to *Sugar Blues*. It is written by a leading nutritionist, and although it's a bit dry, it contains useful information.

Being Fat Is Not a Sin by Shelley Bovey,
Pandora, London, 1989

Written by a journalist who is large and tired of the stigma and discrimination attached to women who are hefty.

Yes!
This is a national magazine that is devoted specifically to large women. They have a very helpful resource directory in the back which lists goods and services for ample-size women. One of the best things is the section that tells you where you can go to find larger-size clothing, either in shops or by mail order. You might have to ask your newsagent to order this magazine for you.

GLOSSARY OF TERMS

acupuncture an ancient Chinese form of treating illness with the use of needles at specific points on the body.

addictive personality a person who tends to be drawn to substances and conditions that become addictive.

aerobic a term that describes exercise which increases the body's oxygen intake.

aetiology the study of causes or beginnings.

allopath term used for doctors who practise traditional medicine.

amphetamine a drug that stimulates the nervous system. A by-product is the loss of appetite.

anaerobic a term that describes exercise which focuses intensely on muscle movements and which cannot be sustained for very long.

anorexia nervosa an eating disorder, the main symptom of which is substantial weight loss.

aromatherapy an alternative health practice that utilises aromatic oils for balancing the body and emotions.

assertiveness the art of expressing needs and desires without being aggressive.

bulimia an eating disorder that is typified by overeating and then vomiting.

candida (or **candida albicans**) a yeast-like organism (fungus) present to some degree in the intestinal walls of all humans. When this fungus grows excessively, a host of vague symptoms and feelings of general ill health can be experienced.

deprivation mentality a term I use to indicate the state of feeling needy because of the rigid restrictions that continual dieting demands.

endorphin a hormone released within the brain that gives a feeling of well-being.

enzyme a substance that acts as a catalyst in the digestion of food.

exorphin   a protein substance that has an opiate-like effect.

homeostasis   a state of equilibrium, no fluctuations.

homeopathic   a form of alternative medicine that uses the concept of like curing like.

hyperplastic obesity   a term used to denote someone who has become overweight before they have reached their physical maturity.

hypertrophic obesity   a term used to denote someone who became overweight as an adult.

iridologist   a complementary medicine practitioner who uses the eyes as the indicator of illness.

mantra   a word or group of words that is repeated frequently to focus a person's attention. Generally used in meditation.

meditate   the act of quieting the mind and focusing the attention by sitting in a quiet and undisturbed place.

mouth hunger   a term I use to indicate an urge to eat that is not the result of actual physical hunger or the body's need for food. It is a psychological desire to eat.

naturopathic   a natural method of healing without the use of drugs, chemicals or artificial substances.

Oedipal history   early childhood history information obtained by looking at the relationship with the parents.

placebos   medicines with no chemical or medical components, generally made of sugar.

pre-verbal   referring to a time in the development of the human being before the use of speech.

psychic   a dimension of the human being in which things are known or felt intuitively.

purging   getting rid of food that has been ingested, either by using laxatives or vomiting it back up.

putrefication   foods ferment and become rancid in the stomach or the bowel when they have not been digested properly.

set point   the natural weight that the body automatically assumes if left to itself to balance out.

subclinical eating disorder   a new term used to describe a condition in which people who constantly concerned about their weight and are continually trying to alter it. Their eating behaviour is not as exaggerated as those who are considered clinically eating disordered.

toxaemia   the state of being full of a substance or conditions that are toxic to the body.

treatment milieu   the particular philosophy and approach used in the course of a treatment programme.

INDEX

ectomorphic 144, 149
as emotional mirror 47–8
endomorphic 140, 148–9
energy flow 48
exercise 161
influence of mind on 153–4
learning to love your body 34–5
mesomorphic 144, 149
and overeating 48
questionnaire on attitude to 30
relaxation 110
as rhythmic cycle 134–5
set point 185, 200
size discrimination 76
bulimia 5
described 8
Eating Disorders Association
194
recovery from 182
and stable weight 79
statistics 9
symptoms 9

calories 38, 121, 129, 165–6
candida 130, 199
Centre for the Study of
Complementary Medicine
193
change, and relationship with
others 118
children 58, 69, 80
Christmas 164–5
clients' experiences
a baby with a pregnant mother
64
Christmas T-shirt 164
craving for peppermint 127
dieting and exercise 156–7
eating 82
eating and dieting 45

emotional dilemma and
unsuccessful attempts at
weight loss 111–12
husband sabotaging weight loss
46
innocuous remarks with long-
lasting effects 67–8
lack of compassion for self 101
obesity 138–9
pregnancy and overweight 75–6
reason for feeling of inadequacy
65
self-consciousness 97–8
sugar consumption 130–1
weight loss 25–6
clothes 170, 179, 197
Complementary Medicine Services
193–4
compulsive eating
anxiety and 36
breaking the habit of 115, 119
Christmas 166
common characteristics of
compulsive eaters 99–102
cycle of overeating 87–90
defined 86
dieting and 22, 26
done unconsciously 36
Eating Disorders Association
194
feelings of failure and
inadequacy 76
help available 17, 18
honesty with oneself over 37
overeaters and exercise 159
and piggy-backing problems 94,
96
recovering from 176–7, 182,
185
self-esteem and 97